ALMA MAHLER

ALMA MAHLER

or
the Art of Being Loved

FRANÇOISE GIROUD

Translated by
R. M. STOCK

Oxford   New York
OXFORD UNIVERSITY PRESS
1991

Oxford University Press, Walton Street, Oxford OX2 6DP
Oxford New York Toronto
Delhi Bombay Calcutta Madras Karachi
Petaling Jaya Singapore Hong Kong Tokyo
Nairobi Dar es Salaam Cape Town
Melbourne Auckland
and associated companies in
Berlin Ibadan

Oxford is a trade mark of Oxford University Press

Published in the United States
by Oxford University Press, New York

British Library Cataloguing in Publication Data
data available

Library of Congress Cataloging in Publication Data
Giroud, Françoise.
[Alma Mahler, ou, L'art d'être aimeé. English]
Alma Mahler, or, The art of being loved / Françoise Giroud:
translated by R.M. Stock.
Translation of: Alma Mahler, or, L'art d'être aimée.
Includes bibliographical references and index.
1. Mahler, Alma, 1879–1964. 2. Vienna (Austria)—Biography.
3. Wives—Biography. 4. Mahler, Gustav, 1860–1911.
5. Gropius, Walter, 1883–1969. 6. Werfel, Franz, 1890–1945.
7. Arts—Austria—History—20th century. I. Title.
DB844.M34G5713 1991 780'.92–dc20 [B]
ISBN 0–19–816156–5

Set by Hope Services (Abingdon) Ltd.
Printed in Great Britain by
Bookcraft (Bath) Ltd.,
Midsomer Norton, Avon

CONTENTS

LIST OF ILLUSTRATIONS

1. A Goddess who made Gods of her Lovers

'It's Alma's last mad fling', said Franz Werfel, her husband. This time—the year was 1934—the object of her attentions was a priest, the theologian Johannes Hollnsteiner. He was 38, she was 55. Rumour had it that he would be the next cardinal of Vienna after Monsignor Innitzer.

A platonic relationship? All the evidence points to the contrary. It was certainly intense. 'You are the first and you'll be the last', said the reverend father, fascinated by this sensuous penitent who in the past few months had surprised herself with her own religious fervour. And she was not a woman to go for confession to the local parish priest.

Every day after mass, which she now suddenly attended regularly, she rejoined him in his apartment. In the afternoon, the reverend father's limousine was parked outside her house. Before suppressing references to her relationship with Hollnsteiner in her private diary—she made a habit of such self-censorship—she had noted: 'My whole being asks for nothing but to submit to him, but I must resist my own desires. He is the first man who has ever conquered me.'

The first? Admittedly, every new love affair effaces the ones before, but the woman who wrote those words had been wife to Gustav Mahler, mistress to Oskar Kokoschka, wife to Walter Gropius, and was now married to Franz Werfel. Music, painting, architecture, literature—an impressive handful of aces, even if posterity does not rate Werfel's work as highly as that of the three men who had preceded him in Alma's toils. In his day Werfel was considered the equal of Thomas Mann.

But it is true that she had always done the conquering. And then what? Mahler had died, perhaps through loving her too much, Kokoschka never resigned himself to having lost her, Gropius had been a toy to play with when it pleased her, and Werfel wrote: 'She is one of the very few sorceresses of our time . . . '.

Creative artists are probably no more difficult to seduce than plumbers, the problem is meeting them. And circumstances were such that Alma always lived among them. But once she had caught them, they could not get away. It was she who was unfaithful, she who broke things off, she who did the divorcing. She was not one of those women who, once wooed and won, become an encumbrance. Their conquest of her was never complete, that was where her power lay. She drew her strength from the image she had of herself as a member of the élite, a precious object, a superior being. And by any objective standard, she was out of the ordinary. When she appeared, her radiant presence magnetically attracted all eyes as she moved like a queen around the room. Men drowned in the startling blue of her eyes. Intelligent into the bargain, with a fine, demanding intelligence, her interests were wide, she was sometimes mordant and could be profound.

At 20 this fair-haired beauty had been nourished on Nietzsche, Wagner, and Plato. Later she was to learn Greek and translate the Fathers of the Church. She also wrote music. Composition was of all her activities the one she took most seriously. Music was her natural element.

No, she was certainly not just anybody, this young woman around whom men never ceased to buzz. But one can be exceptional and still be dissatisfied with oneself. Indeed, that is the general rule. Alma, however, had the feeling that she really was a perfect example of a superior human being, and it is clear that this feeling never left her, even when age began to spoil her beauty. This lofty idea of herself, so rare in women, this satisfied awareness of herself which shows in all her writing, was one of her striking characteristics.

She was aware of only one blemish, a minute one, which caused her all her life to avoid gatherings where there were too many people. A childhood illness had left her deaf in one ear. But this minor handicap had become an additional source of attraction. In conversation she listened so intently that she gave the other person the impression that on one else existed for her.

Once a man had attracted her because she had detected in him the thing that always fascinated her, talent (Alma reacted to talent like some women do to money), she began immediately to exaggerate his qualities. An exceptional woman like her, she felt, could be attracted only by an exceptional man. She surrounded him with his aura, exalted his gifts, endowed him with superhuman energy. Alma was a goddess who made a god of each of her lovers.

The harder they fell when she knocked them off their pedestals. What poor things they were then, without her!

All the same, in one respect her life was a failure. With or without her, her men would have made a lasting impression on the world: Mahler's cathedrals of sound, Gropius's tubular steel constructions, Werfel's novels, Kokoschka's unruly paintings. She, without them, would have been nothing. They left behind what they had created, the only traces she left were of herself on them, scars branded deep into their flesh. The usual fate of women of her time? No doubt, but in her case the waste involved was something out of the ordinary.

This man-hungry beauty, this lioness tormented by illusions of fame, had great musical ability. We have said that she composed: by the age of 20 she had already written more than a hundred Lieder, some instrumental pieces, and the outline of an opera. She clearly had a vocation for a career in music other than making copies of her husband's scores.

Forbidden to compose by Mahler ('From now on you have only one job: to make me happy!'), she obeyed. But at what a cost to both of them! Some sacrifices bring deep satisfaction to those who have that kind of temperament. No one was less made for self-sacrifice than Alma. To be a handmaiden to genius, and find satisfaction in it, was not the job for Alma. She did it with feelings of frustration and sometimes despair, for, by an irony of fate, Alma made her sacrifice for a man whose music she did not like. Who can say whether the world of art lost anything of consequence as a result? Most of her works have disappeared. But that does not really answer the question.

2. Vienna, in Flight from Reality

What was there then about the Viennese that made their city unique for so long, until it sank into the Fascist night, to emerge exhausted from the Second World War a prosaic, provincial city remarkable only for its many museums? Lightheartedness, conviviality, amused self-mockery, casualness, gaiety, unconcern, irony, a love of pleasure, a gift for joyous celebration, a liking for rich food, a cultivated refinement . . . And an occasional spark of eroticism, according to Arthur Koestler.

In 1902 Rodin, who had come to see the Secession exhibition in which the painter Klimt was showing his Beethoven frieze, was invited to a garden party in the Prater, Vienna's most celebrated park. The women were exquisite, the weather mild, someone went to the piano and played Schubert. Rodin said to Klimt: 'I have never felt like this before . . . Your frieze, so tragic and yet so serene . . . the exhibition, unforgettable . . . And then the garden, the women, the music and everywhere and in everyone such joyous naïvety . . . I find it captivating!'

A journalist, Berta Zuckerkandl, translated this for Klimt who replied simply: 'Österreich!' Austria. Life was such fun! Vienna, on the Danube, was almost as large a city as Paris, but it merged more harmoniously with the gentle wooded hills of the surrounding countryside. The Viennese went from masked balls to festive parties, all sections of the population meeting and mingling. During Fasching (the Carnival, Shrove Tuesday) the whole city danced—and during the rest of the year too, for that matter—to the waltzes of Johann Strauss and the melodies of Franz Lehar, whose operettas were drawing the crowds into the theatres. Music was the favourite pastime of the Viennese, so much so that they had been obliged to ban the playing of instruments after 11 p.m.

An intense social life was carried on in the cafés which seemed to be on every street and corner. Everyone had his favourite café in which he and his friends were 'regulars'. There they read the Viennese and foreign newspapers, had their mail delivered to them, played chess, and, above all, talked. They were great talkers. Nothing was ever decided, no conclusions were ever reached, everything was smoke, play on words, flashes of humour, intellectual castles in the air, metaphysical discussions . . . And all this was a male preserve.

It was a café, the Griensteidl, which served as the headquarters of 'Young Vienna', a small group of intellectuals which included Arthur Schnitzler and Hugo von Hofmannsthal. The journalist Karl Kraus, the most hated man in Vienna, also dined there every evening. At the Café Louvre, Theodor Herzl, the inventor of the Jewish State, brought together the first Zionists. At the Café Central the social democrats met, and Trotsky played chess every evening. At the Imperial, Mahler was to be seen scrutinizing the newspapers the morning after a première. And, after the Griensteidl had been demolished, the poets met at the Herrendorf. In 'a secure world in which any radical transformation, any violent change seemed unthinkable' (Stefan Zweig), in which society was advancing smoothly along what was believed to be the road of progress, the Viennese *Kaffeehaus* was the most solid of institutions.

While the beautiful Empress Elizabeth journeyed restlessly all over Europe, Franz Josef of Habsburg reigned, from the *Hofburg* and from his palace at Schönbrunn, over a mosaic of peoples—Croats and Serbians, Czechs, Germans, Italians, Magyars, Poles, Romanians, Ruthenians, Slovaks, Slovenes—with their conflicting nationalisms, their claims for independent statehood, their Pan-Slav or Greater German ideas, a hotchpotch of contradictions which he took care not to try to resolve, since any solution would have meant the end of the empire. So he compromised, and everything seemed to be holding together. To worry about those things would have required a taste for anticipating the future, which was the last thing the Viennese would indulge in, perhaps because it would have spoilt their enjoyment of life.

Of all the emperor's subjects, the Jews of the Viennese bourgeoisie, completely 'assimilated', were the most loyal. It had all begun in 1867 when freedom of religion and conscience, the sign of emancipation, was written into the Constitution. From then onwards symbiosis had occurred, as in Spain in the fifteenth century. Since the Jews had no chance whatsoever of making a career in the army or the higher ranks of the civil service, they turned to the liberal professions and industry, and occupied a strong position in the financial aristocracy. The great liberal Viennese newspaper, the *Neue Freie Presse*, belonged to a Jewish family, the Benedikts. As liberals they supported the emperor and the multinational state because that was the guarantee of their security. What would have happened if the empire had broken up? The Jews constituted a people—the official history of the monarchy referred to them as such—but unlike the other peoples of the empire they had no territory they could call their own. Multinational liberalism was therefore their safeguard.

Jews and non-Jews alike, all the Viennese made use, in dealing with the imperial bureaucracy, of the backstairs influence known as *Protektion*—for business reasons, for personal promotion, or for obtaining a post. Even Freud used it. Everyone knew someone who knew someone who knew someone.

An outstanding characteristic of Viennese life was the importance attached to art. An extreme form of sensual aestheticism was cultivated there, and in Vienna alone of European capitals this was something shared by all sections of society. The phenomenon was so powerful and so original, if one compares Vienna with Paris, London, or Berlin, that it demands closer investigation.

According to the sociologist Carl E. Schorske, the explanation was as follows: culture was the way chosen by the Viennese middle classes to put themselves on the same footing as the aristocracy, which they had been neither able to destroy, as elsewhere, nor to gain access to. Between the imperial aristocracy, which provided the army officers and the higher ranks of the civil service, and what was called in Vienna 'the second society', that is to say the élite of the middle classes (bankers, industrialists, members of the liberal professions, intellectuals, and artists) there were neither contacts nor exchanges. At the most, an eligible daughter with a generous dowry might sometimes break through the barrier surrounding the 'first' society.

But the Viennese bourgeoisie, energetic, wealthy, individualistic, liberal, had made its entry into history. Through architecture it had recorded that entry in stone: the extensive construction work of the 1860s which had completely remodelled the city around a circular boulevard in its centre, the Ring, fringed with monuments and grandiose mansions, was the seal the bourgeoisie had set on the imperial capital. Through patronage, which it extended to all the arts, the bourgeoisie took over the most ancient of aristocratic traditions, and did it in the grand manner. When the artists of the Secession were looking for a place to exhibit modern art, it was the industrialist Karl Wittgenstein, the father of the philosopher, who provided the bulk of the funds for a new building. When in 1903 the architect Josef Hoffmann and the versatile artist Kolo Moser conceived the idea of the Wiener Werkstätten, workshops for craftsmen designed 'to arouse the interest of the masses in a refined modern style', it was the industrialist Fritz Wärndorfer who financed them, up until 1914.

The bourgeoisie also generously supported theatrical and musical activities, which they adored. 'The first thing we look at on opening our newspapers', said Stefan Zweig, 'is the list of public entertainments.' The glorification of culture in all its manifestations was such that Vienna was probably the only city in the world where fathers rejoiced when their sons decided to devote their lives to music or literature. The case of Arthur Schnitzler's father, a doctor, who was furious when he learnt that his son was giving up his own medical practice to devote himself to the theatre, was so exceptional that it became the talk of the town. He got over his disappointment, however, at the first night of the *Liebelei*. The father of Hugo von Hofmannsthal (*Der Rosenkavalier*, *Elektra*), on the other hand, was a splendid example of the traditional attitude of the bourgeoisie; he gave his son an upbringing specifically designed to teach him to enjoy the pleasures of the mind.

Finally, Vienna was the only city in the world in which artists and intellectuals made no attempt to revolt against the bourgeois élite. On the contrary, they remained for a long time perfectly integrated with it. Together they formed a coherent and complete stratum of society in which everyone knew everyone else, and all were united in cultivating 'art for art's sake'.

Whatever the historical origins of this attitude might have been, by the end of the century it had taken on the character of a flight from reality. At that time, people in Europe—not only in Vienna—still believed that man was a rational being who would acquire mastery over nature through science, and mastery over himself through moral rectitude. He would thus be able to build a just society, a process which had indeed already begun. That was the basic credo of the liberalism which had governed Austria since the 1860s.

It was known that there were malcontents, especially among the peasants, artisans, and workers, and that the Social Democrats, the Christian Social Party, the pan-Germanists, and the Slav nationalists had formed political parties, but nothing seemed to threaten the established authority of an appointed government guided by but not necessarily reflecting a Parliament resulting from free elections with restricted suffrage.

There was alarm in Vienna on 1 May 1890 when the socialists, red carnations in their buttonholes, marched through the Prater in serried ranks of four. To everyone's surprise the demonstrators did not break any windows or loot shops. They marched on out under the lush greenery of the Nobelallee singing the Internationale. And everyone breathed again.

And then, in 1895, the storm broke. The municipal elections in Vienna resulted in a landslide victory for the Christian Social Party. The leader of the party, Karl Lueger, a militant anti-Semite, had succeeded in gaining the support of the pan-Germanist movement, led by another virulent anti-Semite, Schönerer. Both of them were powerful influences in Hitler's political apprenticeship.

Could Lueger be the master of Vienna? The emperor imposed his veto and refused to ratify the election results. And Freud smoked a cigar to celebrate the attitude of the autocrat before whom, as a young man, he had refused to take off his hat! Franz Josef, who detested anti-Semitism and had no particular liking for the municipal socialism preached by Lueger, held out for two years. Some of his ministers tried in vain to get the Vatican to disown the Catholic leader.

But when in subsequent elections the Viennese confirmed their choice, the emperor had to give in. In 1897 Karl Lueger, whose anti-Semitism was a matter of tactics ('whether someone is a Jew or not is a matter for me to decide'), became Bürgermeister of Vienna. Good-looking with his full blond beard, an efficient manager, basing his propaganda on the defence of the little man, he was someone to be reckoned with. He was one of the first great demagogues of modern times. Politics had hitherto been a matter for negotiation between élites. Lueger was the first to apply to it the mobilization of the masses.

At the subsequent legislative elections, the liberal party lost seats throughout the whole country. And they were never to recover the ground they lost. How did the Viennese bourgeoisie, liberals from time immemorial, react? Initially shocked, bewildered, suddenly made aware of the harsh realities of social conditions, they simply turned their backs on the question and took refuge in cultural activities. Electoral failure having revealed the liberals' lack of power, they concluded that political action was no longer worthwhile. They lost interest in public affairs, abandoned their duties as active citizens, and threw themselves into art as a substitute for action, something which would give their lives a sense of direction. They chose aestheticism as a cure for the wounds inflicted by politics.

Was this a desperate delaying strategy in the face of the onward march of history, or the defence of the true way of life against the forces of death? Or was it an elegant attempt 'to bow out of the real world', a veritable genius for resorting to hedonism as a means of evading all moral problems? Someone coined a phrase which was to become symbolic of the Viennese attitude to life: the situation is hopeless, but not serious.

This drifting away from the real world—*das Gleitende* as Hofmannsthal called it—was accompanied by a growing obsession with subjectivity, a preoccupation with introspection, exploration of the world of the mind, intuition of a conflict between traditional moral values and psychological realities. At the turn of the century the time had come for Freud to reveal to mankind that it was not governed by reason but by two obscure forces, Eros and Thanatos. Nevertheless, citizen of Vienna that he was, the good doctor belatedly got himself registered on the electoral roll in 1908.

As for Arthur Schnitzler, the only entry relating to public affairs in his diary was the following: 'We even talked about politics.' That was in 1897. Hofmannsthal, noting that alarm at the liberals' defeat had engendered a growing passion for art, concluded: 'We must say goodbye to a world before it falls about our ears. Many people already realize this, and a mysterious unease makes them all become poets.'

At the same time, culture became an instrument of government, the attitude of the state reflecting the change in the attitude of the public. In high places art was perceived as a means of transcending nationality, culture as the field in which the various nationalisms could meet and in which it could be meaningful to say one was Austrian.

It was in this climate of 'joyful apocalypse', as Hermann Broch described it, of art raised to a supreme value, the symbolic cement of the multinational empire, that Alma grew up. It would be impossible to understand her in any other context.

To complete this rapid picture, something must be said about the situation of women in Viennese society at the turn of the century, that is to say when Alma was just 20 years old. Some Viennese women had a recognized place in society similar to that of certain French women in the eighteenth century. Vienna had feminized culture as, in other times, Paris had done. Berta Zuckerkandl (mentioned earlier) received artists and intellectuals every Sunday in her apartment with its Josef Hoffmann decor. Countess Nora Wydenbruck, Ida Bonrat, the wife of the industrialist Karl Reininghaus, and many others held their salons. Women lived more freely than in France. Some even smoked in public. Alma went unaccompanied to her music lessons.

Nevertheless, girls were brought up to regard their virginity as something sacrosanct, prudery was the rule, hysterical breakdowns were frequent. Men, single or not, went to obtain from actresses or working girls what the women of their own milieu longed to give them but could not, for their honour stood in the way. A respectable woman, in Vienna as elsewhere, did not possess a body. If she discovered she did have one, then the devil must have got into the holy water. Once her sexuality was aroused, the irrepressible violence of her instincts, her natural propensity to lewdness, would be unleashed. Women had to be defended against themselves, by education and constraint. And it was from them, insatiable women with thighs outspread, that men must be protected if they were not to lose the best of themselves. For a lustful woman diverted a man from the intellectual preoccupations of which he had the monopoly, she distracted his energies from superior accomplishments, she was the natural enemy of morality, reason, and creativity.

In a loudly acclaimed book published in 1903, *Sex and Character*, Otto Weininger, a young philosopher of 23, pushed to the limits of delirium this heroic vision of virility as opposed to abject femininity, synonym for abandonment to the blind instincts of primitive nature. Weininger, who had a touch of genius, put forward a further postulate: that all human beings were bisexual, carriers of the twin elements of virility and femininity. He was the first to write about this. Freud and Fliess criticized him moreover for having filched this discovery from confidential conversations. 'He opened the castle with a stolen key', Freud said later.

But Weininger did not draw from his brilliant discovery the conclusions one might have hoped for. Noting what he called the feminization of society which, according to him, sapped the virile values, denouncing in one and the same breath the Mother and the Whore, the two faces of the principle of decay, he hit out at 'amoral and lascivious' women with unprecedented violence.

While he was at it he contrived, by analogy, to put the Jews in the dock alongside them. Declaring that what he called typically feminine behaviour—dishonesty, materialism, trickery—was the result of the interiorization of centuries of oppression, he attributed to the Jews the same characteristics for the same reasons, and vented his spleen on them too.

Having spoken, Otto Weininger (a Jew himself) committed suicide. He was 23, and before he died he wrote: 'I think I have given the final answer to the so-called feminine question.' An ambitious claim. The issue in question was certainly burning deep in the heart of Viennese society.

But things were moving. In 1897, a woman was accepted into the Faculty of Medicine for the first time. Rosa Mayderer, daughter of an upper middle-class family, founded the Association of Austrian Women. With the help of her husband, an architect, she calmly demanded new rights for women—and urged them to take up bicycling! Nothing, she felt, would advance the cause of emancipation more. In an essay entitled 'Sex and Culture' she firmly rebutted Otto Weininger's theories.

New ideas were beginning to spread as to what relationships

should be between a couple made up of equal partners. But to say what such relationships should be was one thing, to live them out another. Arthur Schnitzler, the clever dandy, was one of those caught on the horns of this dilemma. 'What I would like most would be a harem, and not to be disturbed.'

As for Mahler, after his engagement to Alma he wrote to her: 'Don't misunderstand me. Don't go thinking that I take the bourgeois view that a wife is a kind of plaything for her husband, and also his housekeeper. Can you really believe I would think that?' And, indeed, that was not what he thought. Mahler was no ordinary man. What he expected of her went well beyond that. 'You must subordinate every detail of your future life to my needs, and want only my love in return.' He asked her 'simply' to become part of him, forgetting all her own desires, ambitions, and dreams.

In demanding this he was speaking as the creative genius who must sweep aside anything that might disturb or impede his activity. This is indeed something that creative artists seldom fail to do. Mahler had the invincible strength of those who are convinced that they are engaged in major creative work and who are sustained by that conviction against all difficulties, misunderstandings, tauntings, and set-backs. 'I would like to attend the first performance of my symphony in fifty years' time', he said, after one of his works had been badly received. Secretly, he believed that one day he would be played as often as Beethoven. Secretly, he believed he was Beethoven.

The trouble was that Alma did not believe in his genius. What she admired in Mahler was his prowess as a conductor, as director of the Opera, as the 'star' (as we should say today) whom she went to listen to almost every evening. When finally she met him, the time they spent at a dinner together was more than she needed to make him fall in love with her.

3. The Forming of Alma

So far, Alma had had flirtations that had sometimes gone further than they should. She was the daughter of a landscape painter of repute, Emil Jakob Schindler, and a minor singer, Anna Bergen, who had given up her own career to devote herself to her husband. After a difficult start, Schindler had been plucked from obscurity by wealthy patrons, his material worries had vanished, orders had poured in, and for the rest of his life he had lived in fine style in a romantic castle on the outskirts of Vienna in which he gave one sumptuous party after another.

Alma worshipped this delightful father who read Goethe to her when she was 8 years old. She had nothing but contempt for her mother, who seems nevertheless to have been a charming, though somewhat fickle, person.

A younger sister, Grete, more retiring by nature, was to meet a tragic end. After a happy marriage, she made several attempts at suicide. She was put in an asylum. Alma then extracted the truth from her mother. Grete was not Schindler's daughter, but the fruit of a short-lived love affair Anna had had with a man who had probably been syphilitic, like so many of his contemporaries. After the *Anschluss*, the Nazis put Grete to death with the rest of the mentally sick.

As children, the two sisters got on well together. The family was living a life of luxury and comfort when Emil Schindler suddenly died, during a journey with his family, of an obstruction of the intestinal tract. Alma was 13 years old. The shock was terrible.

After the delay demanded by convention, Anna married again, this time Schindler's disciple and assistant Carl Moll, a fair-haired giant who had been her lover. The adolescent Alma was outraged. 'You don't marry the pendulum when you've had the whole clock', she wrote. She found it hard to forgive her mother for this 'come-down'. But Carl Moll was by no means the colourless character Alma took him for when she treated him with disdain and refused to accord him the slightest parental authority. He was a talented painter whose knowledge and acumen enabled him later to play a leading role in Viennese artistic life and the market for art.

At 17, Alma had never been to school except for a few months, and had only received a vague religous education, but she knew Wagner by heart. She had even spoilt a pretty mezzo-soprano voice by singing the whole of the Wagnerian repertory which she adored. She had studied counterpoint, was a voracious student of scores, had tried her hand at sculpture, and above all had read widely.

One of her father's friends, Max Burckhard, an eminent jurist and influential man of the theatre who had brought Ibsen's plays to Vienna, directed her reading. He put together a library of classics and sent it to her, one Christmas Eve, in two enormous hampers. She had even read Stendhal, and above all Nietzsche, whom Burckhard recommended to her and of whom she became a devotee. The 'superman' concept suited her to perfection.

Burckhard formed her mind, chaperoned her, took her to the Mozart Festival at Salzburg, to the theatre, to the Opera. He was twenty-five years her senior. He would have been a perfect father-substitute, if his fondness for her had not ultimately gone beyond reasonable limits. She was taunting, hurtful. He went off in a huff, came back again. 'His vigorous manhood intrigues me', she noted in her diary. Intrigued, flattered, but untroubled, she made fun of him.

It was Gustav Klimt, 'the prince of painters', who first aroused her. 'Reach for the stars', her father had told her. Klimt was to be the first of them. He was a frequent visitor at the Molls' house. With Carl Moll and a third painter, Josef Engelhardt, he had conceived a plan to hive off ('secede') from the artistic establishment in Vienna. The idea of the Secession was to break with the prevailing Viennese academicism still dominated by the facile expert in pictorial beauty, Makart, and purely and simply to revolutionize all the plastic and decorative arts. This ambitious project took shape at meetings in Berta Zuckerkandl's salon.

Berta was a well-known figure in Vienna. Daughter of a great journalist, journalist herself, married to a famous professor of anatomy, Emil Zuckerkandl, linked already in her 'teens with Georges Clemenceau, the French statesman, who on occasion entrusted her with political missions, Berta was a tall, exuberant, dark-haired young woman, then about 30 years of age, who played hostess to everyone who was anyone in the artistic circles of the capital. At the behest of her friends she organized countless meetings and working sessions between all those—whether painters, architects, or decorators—who seemed likely to join forces with Klimt and Moll.

The Secession had forty founder members. They elected Klimt as their president. The second 'period' of that virtuoso painter, so utterly representative of his epoch, was about to begin. But the Secessionists needed a place to exhibit. The official exhibition building, the *Künstlerhaus*, was not open to contemporary art. So they cast around, canvassed for funds, sought for a wealthy patron. Moll, a good organizer, took charge of the practical arrangements.

The *Kunsttempel*, built by Josef Maria Olbrich in six months on the basis of a sketch by Klimt, was in itself revolutionary. The whole building rested on six pillars, and its internal walls were movable. Its pediment displayed the motto of the Secession: 'To each epoch its art, to art its freedom'. The Secession also brought out a review, *Ver Sacrum*. And Klimt, now a friend of the Moll household, fell under Alma's spell.

She was 17 years old and, in her own words, 'a beautiful God-fearing maiden'. Klimt, 35, had no particular intellectual pretentions but was an outstanding artist. As a landscape painter, and creator of frescos in the decorative style of Makart (up to 1880 the dominant influence in Viennese taste in all branches of art), Klimt had already acquired a considerable reputation.

He was a man of few words, fair-haired with a matt complexion behind a fringe beard. He dressed in loose-fitting monks' robes for comfort, and would often go out of his way to be provocative. Above all, in a city where malicious gossip was raised to the status of an eighth art, everyone knew and went round saying that he cohabited with a fashionable dressmaker, Emilie Flöge. In a society so concerned with conformity to convention, Klimt was regarded as excessively original.

Frau Moll decided accordingly to put an end to her daughter's obvious liking for him, and the family left for Italy. Klimt promptly went after them, and followed them from town to town. The Molls put up with him until one day Frau Moll, leafing through her daughter's diary, discovered an account of a certain kiss. She ordered Klimt to go, once and for all. The result was a series of furtive rendezvous in the streets of Venice where Alma managed to evade her mother's supervision, passionate vows were exchanged, Klimt swore he would kidnap Alma, she promised to follow him . . .

Back in Vienna she saw him again, and only managed to resist an invitation to visit his studio because she wished to preserve that precarious asset, her virginity! Then Carl Moll intervened and forbade Klimt to enter his house until further orders. Klimt was utterly crushed. In a long, moving letter he pleaded not guilty: 'Alma is beautiful, intelligent, witty, she has everything a man can wish for in a woman, and in abundant measure. I believe that wherever she appears in the world of men she is mistress, sovereign . . . Can't you understand that there are moments when one loses control of one's thoughts and becomes confused with regard to her?' He gave in, nevertheless. He valued Moll's friendship and did not wish to lose it. Alma, for her part, submitted in despair. What else could they do?

After an interval, the painter and the young girl met again in the home of mutual friends. Klimt behaved correctly, but for the rest of his life he felt for Alma that special tenderness which only frustrated love can bring. After this episode, which coincided with the opening months of the Secession, the prince of painters pursued his brilliant career. In his new manner he seemed to be striving to grasp the very essence of femininity, showing against gold-leaf backgrounds visions of dreamy, sinuous, soft-fleshed women with tapering hands and long, floating hair—so sweet, so perverse, so dangerous. Klimt in his paintings was echoing Freud.

And then came the scandal. The Minister of Education had commissioned from the painter three large paintings for the ceiling of the entrance hall of the university, on the themes of Philosophy, Medicine, Jurisprudence. When the pictures were exhibited, they provoked violent protests. Eighty-seven professors signed a petition requesting the minister not to allow them to be mounted in the university. Emil Zuckerkandl, then doyen of the Faculty of Medicine, stood up for Klimt, but his was a solitary voice. The 'Medicine' painting—with a nude female figure on the left of the picture and a pregnant woman—was considered to be an outrage to public morality, while Klimt's representation of 'Philosophy' was, to put it mildly, disturbing. Furious, Klimt declared that he would reimburse the fees he had received, and keep his paintings. The affair took a political turn, and Education Minister Wilhelm von Hartel was questioned in Parliament. A Christian-Social deputy asked how the government could 'tolerate such an abuse of art which threatened young people's morality by means of obscene pictures'. The government refused to accept the reimbursement of fees by the painter and demanded that the pictures should be handed over to the Ministry's officials. Klimt refused to comply. When the lorry appeared in front of his house to take away the three paintings, he shouted: 'I shall shoot anyone who tries to come in! Tell that to the minister!'

In the end it was the government which gave way. But the violence of the controversy and the ugly turn it had taken gave Klimt an aversion to allegorical, 'committed' subjects. From then until his death in 1918, his main activity was painting portraits on commission of the pretty young women of Viennese society. The three frescoes were destroyed in 1945 in Schloss Innendorf, when the castle was burnt down by the Nazis.

Klimt had one admirer, however, in the person of Hitler who, as is known, had certain painterly ambitions himself. In the late 1930s the Führer asked for an exhibition of Klimt's work to be organized. A number of portraits were assembled for him. 'Who is that?' he asked, 'and that one, and that one there?' A number of Jewish names were mentioned. Hitler cancelled the exhibition.

Klimt's successor in Alma's affections was a composer whose works are now beginning to be performed again: Alexander von Zemlinsky. She drove him to distraction. She allowed him to kiss her, caress her, indulge in every intimacy except the ultimate. She talked of getting engaged, then refused to consider marriage, blew hot, then cold, exchanged passionate letters with him. She tortured him for two years. He was her music teacher.

He was remarkably ugly ('a hideous gnome' according to Alma) but his eyes sparkled with intelligence, and, like all the people she chose to cultivate, there was something out of the ordinary about him. At 25, spurred on by the encouragements the ageing Brahms had heaped upon him, he had written two operas—one, *Es war einmal*, put on by Mahler at the Vienna Opera. He was both a gifted composer and, already, an outstanding teacher. His favourite musical associate, who was later to marry his sister Mathilda, was at that time Arnold Schönberg, whom Alma got to know through him.

As practically the only woman among Zemlinsky's students, Alma was keen to impress, and succeeded in doing so in spite of her teacher's warnings against premature ambitions. But he was soon beyond the admonitory stage. When she failed to appear at his lessons, Zemlinsky went to direct her studies at her home, and they became inseparable.

They did not go out together. Alma was not keen to expose herself to gossip, though she loved to indulge in it herself. When they could not meet, they wrote to each other. Alma's diaries and the hundred or so letters from Zemlinsky which have been preserved give a picture of a stormy relationship in which Alma alternated between bursts of enthusiasm and fits of coldness which drove the young man to despair.

Everything began with music, of course. 'He was playing *Tristan* to me, I leaned over the piano, my knees began to tremble, and we fell into each other's arms . . . '. At first Zemlinsky was dazzled. 'I love you, but you are much too beautiful for me. Men like me may deserve such happiness, but it never comes to them . . . '. Later: 'No one ever loved anyone as much as I love you'.

She kept on asking him whether he had had a physical relationship with a woman who was reputed to have been his mistress. He confessed that he had, whereupon Alma gave vent to a tirade of retrospective jealousy. Pathological jealousy was part of her nature. The unique, the incomparable goddess Alma could not bear the thought that another woman had occupied, however fleetingly, the thoughts, the heart, the senses of someone who now claimed to love her. Not only did she take it for granted that he must be totally hers in the present, and that the slightest friendship, the slightest liking of which she was not the object was an affront to her. She also wanted there to have been no rival in the past.

Zemlinsky redoubled his protestations of love for her. She kept on at him to read Nietzsche, which to placate her he finally agreed to do. She then announced to him that she had decided never to marry. He replied that he too did not intend to marry. He humbled himself before her: 'I want to kneel down, kiss the hem of your dress, and worship you as something sacred.'

Within one week two other young men asked for her hand in marriage. One was a certain Felix Muhr. She listened to him, found him 'likeable, distinguished, cultured'—and rich into the bargain. She told Zemlinsky about him. He was devastated.

He was revolted by her cruelty and the pleasure she seemed to take in humiliating him by repeating to him what, allegedly, everyone said about him. Zemlinsky was ugly, Zemlinsky was poor. It was as if she wanted to make him appreciate what the most beautiful girl in Vienna deigned to grant him: the right to love her. He was tired of pleading, weary of waiting for the day when she would agree to be his wife—and why not? Zemlinsky was not just anybody! 'My darling,' he wrote to her, 'have you really so much to give that others must always beg?'

But as soon as he rebelled she tightened the reins again, for she wanted at all costs to keep her music teacher. And with a breathtaking unawareness of inconsistency she complained of giving him more than she received. This theme recurred constantly throughout her life, with each of her men: she was always convinced that they owed her more than they gave, since after all they belonged to her, body and soul!

In the summer of 1901 (Alma was 22 on 31 August) she left with the Molls for a holiday on the Wolfgangsee. Zemlinsky had hoped to be invited too, but in vain. The separation gave rise to a passionate correspondence of which Carl and Anna Moll knew nothing, Zemlinsky's letters containing anodyne pages in which he discussed composition and the books they were both reading, in order to throw the suspicious parents off the scent.

When the young people met again in Vienna, Zemlinsky was at the end of his tether. He knew her now, how he knew her! 'Now I know everything! Your crazy ideas, your boundless vanity, your quest for pleasure!' And since she was always telling him how much he meant to her and that she wanted a child by him, he demanded, as 'proof of love, one hour of happiness' alone with her.

But let Alma speak for herself. Her diary makes interesting reading:

If he does not give himself completely to me, my nerves will suffer torture. But if he does give himself *completely*, the consequences will be dreadful. The one is as dangerous as the other. I madly desire his embraces, I shall never forget the feel of his hand deep in my innermost self like a torrent of flames! Such happiness overwhelmed me! So it is true, one can be completely happy! Perfect bliss does exist! I have learnt that in the arms of my beloved. One little [*an illegible word*] more, and I would have been in the seventh heaven. Once again, and he will be completely mine.

I would like to kneel down before him and press my lips to his naked body, kiss everything, everything! Amen!

From which it can be seen that Alma was not a timid prude but burned with fires which were destined, often, to consume her. But she attached a symbolic value to her virginity which far exceeded its real importance. She did not give the young man the 'hour of happiness' he begged for. Besides, she had just met Mahler.

4. Preparation for Tyranny

This time Alma was taking on someone who measured up to her requirements. He had the stature, the ambition, the reputation. And he was twenty years older than she was. In Vienna, where he had been director of the *Hofoper* (the Court Opera) since 1897, he was famous, flattered, reviled, worshipped, attacked. He was a major figure in the life of the city.

He was short, shorter than Alma, vigorous though outwardly frail, vibrant, his body and face never still, exhaustingly irritable. In the Belvedere Gardens where he took his daily walk his fussy deportment amused the children. His devoted friend, the violinist Natalie Bauer Lechner, described him thus: 'He stepped high and struck the ground with his feet like a horse prancing. He proceeded in spurts, now fast, now slow. Sometimes, when he grasped his companion by the hand or by his clothing, he pawed the ground like a wild boar.'

He bit his nails. His voice was deep and powerful, his rages notorious. During such outbursts, his brown eyes flamed behind his thick spectacles, the fine blue veins on his temples stood out, his black mop of hair seemed to stand up on his skull, he crackled, he smouldered, he sparkled, he was frightening. When he laughed, his fine strong mouth revealed very white teeth, his laugh was happy, vibrant, and infectious.

Unlike most of his contemporaries he was clean-shaven and, depending on his mood, which could change from one moment to the next, his face looked very young, or withered and old. His legendary absent-mindedness led him to go out with his hair uncombed and socks hanging around his ankle boots. He was capable of the oddest behaviour and seemed to go out of his way to be tactless.

He ruled the orchestra and singers of the *Hofoper* with an iron hand, achieving style, originality, and grandeur in the midst of innumerable conflicts, some of which were inherent in his function. Others, however, were provoked by his bullying, his despotism, his limitless requirements of precision and quality of sound. The consideration he enjoyed was entirely based on his conducting, and would continue to be so for a long time to come, if not to the end of his life. Hostility, derision, lack of understanding, denigration, torrents of abuse, nothing would be spared him by the opponents of his music wherever it was played, except perhaps in Holland.

The first performance in Vienna of his First Symphony, which took place shortly before he met Alma, was greeted with laughter, catcalls, and a hostile outburst from the press. Alma herself left the hall 'full of anger and resentment' at the composer.

By the autumn of 1901 he had been directing the *Hofoper* for four years, and the results he had obtained, the brilliance of his successes, the quality of the performances offered to the Viennese still imposed some restraint on the animosity of his enemies. But they were always ready to pounce. It was a situation typical of any opera house in any epoch, but it was none the less a constant strain aggravated in Mahler's case by the target he offered to anti-Semitic musicians and newspaper critics.

He had converted to Catholicism in February 1897, an essential preliminary, after Prague, Budapest, and Hamburg, to his obtaining the field marshal's baton which his appointment to the Court Opera at Vienna represented. He did it apparently without soul-searching, as a formality. In his vision of the world and his yearning for a merciful God he was certainly closer to the Christian than the Jewish faith. Alma used to say that he had 'a direct line to God'.

The formality completed, he remained nevertheless the Jew Mahler. His greatest support came from the Court. Fürst Montenuovo, the *Obersthofmeister* (Controller of the Royal Household) was a vigilant protector. In the autumn of 1897 Mahler was promoted from *Kapellmeister* (conductor) to *Direktor* of the *Hofoper*.

Gossip had it, not without some justification, that the director of the Opera had been involved in more than one affair with some of the female singers. He had a particular weakness for sopranos; the most recent one had been Selma Kurz. But he lived with his sister Justi.

He was said to be hopelessly in debt, and it was whispered that he was suffering fron an incurable disease.

He had indeed been seriously ill. Haemorrhoids deep inside his rectum—he called them 'pains in my nether regions'—provoked intestinal bleeding which almost proved fatal. It was not the first attack of this kind he had experienced, but it was the most serious. On the evening of 24 February 1901 he was conducting a performance of *The Magic Flute*, and was obviously in pain. Alma, who had not yet met him, was in the auditorium. When she saw 'that Lucifer face, those pallid cheeks, those glowing eyes', she remarked to her companions, 'No one can carry on for long in that state . . . '.

That night Mahler suffered severe bleeding. Well cared for and operated on (for the third time) by the surgeon Hochenegg to whom the emperor had personally recommended the precious patient, he had slowly recovered. But the feeling he had had of coming close to death had apparently shaken him and changed him much more than the painful physical experience itself.

During the summer, in the house he had just had built at Maiernigg on the Wörthersee, he had been able to work, and his output had been particularly fruitful: eight Lieder, including three of the *Kinder-totenlieder* (Songs for Dead Children), and two movements of the Fifth Symphony. He had left Maiernigg, joking in a letter to a friend about the prolonged sessions he had had to spend in the lavatory, and amusing himself by preparing his own obituary: 'Gustav Mahler has finally been overtaken by the fate he deserved on account of his many monstrous crimes.'

In the autumn he was once more battling away at the *Hofoper*, now with the support of his pupil and ardent disciple, the young conductor Bruno Walter, when Berta Zuckerkandl invited him to dinner. Mahler never went out, never visited anyone in respectable Viennese society, and couldn't bear people he didn't know. But he had got to know Berta by an odd turn of events.

Berta had become sister-in-law to Georges Clemenceau. More precisely, her elder sister Sophie had married Clemenceau's brother Paul. The two sisters and two brothers maintained a very close relationship. Through them there had grown up between Austria and France a sort of cultural and at times political bridge, Sophie's salon in Paris corresponding to Berta's salon in Vienna. Returning from Paris where he had been warmly received at Sophie's, Mahler had telephoned Berta to deliver a message. Still under the spell of Sophie's charm and the understanding welcome given him by the Clemenceaus, he agreed to call and meet Berta. And very soon he was firm friends with her and her husband.

In November 1901 Sophie Clemenceau was passing through Vienna. Berta organized a dinner in her honour and invited Mahler. He accepted on condition that no strangers were present, and added: 'I eat only wholemeal bread and rennet apples.' He had a mania for dieting. 'I know', said Berta.

Some days later the Zuckerkandls met Alma on the Ring and invited her to the dinner. She refused. 'I've been trying for six months to avoid meeting him', she said, referring to Mahler. Mahler cried off at the last moment, a new date was agreed, Berta once more invited Alma, and this time she accepted.

On the evening in question Alma was there, sparkling and radiant, sitting between two of her admirers, Klimt and Max Burckhard, engaged in a lively conversation punctuated by bursts of laughter. Mahler, his curiosity aroused, asked if he might join in. Alma was vivacious, brilliant. After the dinner Mahler manœuvred to be near her when the guests were dispersing into the drawing-room.

Suddenly Berta heard raised voices. She looked round. Alma seemed to have lost her temper, Mahler was stamping impatiently about. 'You have no right to keep for a year a score someone has sent you!' Alma was shouting. 'Especially when the person in question is a real musician like Zemlinsky. He sent you his ballet, you could at least have replied!'

'The ballet is awful!' Mahler replied. 'I don't understand—you're studying music after all—how can you defend such trash?'

'In the first place,' Alma cut in, 'it's not trash. You probably haven't even taken the trouble to look at it. Besides, even if it were bad, you could at least be polite!'

'All right,' said Mahler, holding out his hand to Alma. 'Let's agree on that.' And he promised to see Zemlinsky the very next day.

'Would you like me to explain the symbolism of the libretto?' Alma suggested. The libretto had been written by Hofmannsthal. 'I can't wait to hear your explanation!' said Mahler ironically. 'All right. But first you must explain to me the plot of the *Korean Bride*! She was referring to a particularly absurd ballet then in the repertory at the Opera.

Alma had won. He laughed, asked her questions about her music studies, invited her to show him her work one day, and pressed her to say what day would suit her.

Alma, somewhat embarrassed at having lost her temper, went off to join her friends while Sophie and Berta came over to Mahler. 'It's the first time I've enjoyed being invited out', he told them. He invited them in return to come next day, with Alma, to the dress rehearsal of *The Tales of Hoffmann*, a work he thought highly of.

When Alma came to take her leave, Mahler suggested he should see her home, on foot. She refused, saying that it was late and she preferred to go by cab. He tried to get her to promise to come and see him at the Opera. 'Yes, I will if my work goes well', she replied. 'Word of honour?' asked Mahler.

He left the Zuckerkandl's house with Burckhard, and remarked: 'She is an interesting and intelligent girl. At first I didn't like her and took her for a doll. One doesn't as a rule take seriously girls as young and pretty as she is!' He plied Burckhard with questions about Alma, and got the following response: 'Fräulein Schindler's friends know who she is, the rest don't need to know.' Burckhard could be pretty hateful, with his proprietorial airs. But Mahler didn't mind in the least. He returned home to Auenbruggergasse, walking on air. In a word, he was in love.

As for Alma, she returned home not at all pleased with herself, feeling that in these encounters she had oscillated between shyness due to pride which rendered her utterly unresponsive, and a tendency 'to blurt out everything that came into her mind with an air of self-assurance and audacity'. But that was precisely the secret of her charm. Her pretty features led one to expect her to say silly, obvious things, and nothing of the sort ever passed her lips.

In her diary she summed up her impressions of Mahler as follows: 'I must say I liked him enormously. Of course, he is terribly nervous. He paced around the room like a wild animal. He's pure oxygen. You get burnt if you go too near.'

The following morning Berta and Sophie came to fetch her, and they drove to the Opera. Mahler was waiting impatiently for them. He helped Alma out of her coat, but was so agitated that he forgot to do the same for his other visitors. Indulgently Berta forgave him. 'Love makes one blind, naïve and stupid', she wrote later. And Mahler's infatuation, that morning, was obvious enough.

He offered them a cup of tea in his office. Alma said nothing, but began to rummage through the piles of scores on the piano, while Mahler devoured her with his eyes. 'Fräulein Schindler, did you sleep well?' he asked at last. 'Very well. Why shouldn't I?' 'I didn't sleep a wink all night.'

After this exchange Mahler ushered his guests into the auditorium and took his leave of Alma, reminding her of her promise to come and see him soon. According to her own account, Alma was still not aware of Mahler's greatness, 'the one thing which could make an impression on her'. At that time all she felt for this agitated little man was a certain respect. Which puzzled her somewhat!

The following morning she was still in bed when a note was brought to her. It was a poem, unsigned. The verses were not perhaps of the highest quality, but they certainly carried a message.

> It happened overnight.
> I never would have thought
> That counterpoint and theory of form
> Would trouble my heart again
>
> So all night long
> The rising chorus filled my mind,
> 'Til all the voices merged
> To sing the self-same tune
>
> It happened overnight,
> I stayed wide awake,
> So that, when the knock came,
> My eyes would at once turn to the door.
>
> Now I hear it: Word of honour!*
> Ever and again it sings in my ears—
> A canon of some sort:
> I watch the door—and wait.

Had Mahler forgotten to sign? He was certainly capable of doing so. In any case, Alma had no difficulty in identifying the author. Some

---

* Translator's note. The German expression here rendered by 'word of honour' is 'ein Mann—ein Wort', which means, literally, 'one man—one word'. The expectancy expressed in the poem is heightened thereby.

days later, on 18 November, she was at the Opera with her mother to hear Gluck's *Orfeo*. She looked up towards the director's box. At first Mahler, who was shortsighted, did not recognize her, but then 'he began to flirt in a manner impossible to imagine of a serious man'.

In the interval, Alma and Anna Moll were walking in the foyer when Mahler suddenly appeared. Alma introduced her mother to him. They liked each other at once. Mahler took them into his office. Anna Moll said how pleased she would be to invite him round. Mahler immediately took his large appointments book from a drawer to fix a suitable date, which would have to be after his return from Munich were he was due to conduct the première of his Fourth Symphony.

'Would you take me on as a conductor at the Opera?' Alma asked. 'Yes,' said Mahler, 'I am sure you would do it very well.' 'That doesn't sound like an objective judgement to me!' 'There's no such thing as an objective judgement.' The interval was over. Alma and Mahler parted, both of them moved and convinced 'that something great and beautiful had come into our lives', wrote Alma.

After the performance, the mother and daughter had arranged to have supper with Carl Moll and Max Burckhard. Anna described their encounter with Mahler, and Moll flew into a temper, reproaching his wife for having let Alma set foot in the office of that 'free thinker', that 'artful schemer', an old man, plagued with illness and debts, whose position at the Opera was precarious. 'Besides which he's ugly, and his music isn't much good either', he concluded.

Burckhard, certainly jealous, said to Alma: 'Mahler was quite infatuated with you the other evening. What would you say if he asked you to marry him?'

'I should accept.'

'That would be a sin! You, such a beauty and of such a good family. Don't throw all that away on a rachitic, degenerate Jew. Think of your children—it would be a sin! Besides, fire and water could perhaps manage to get on, but not fire with fire. You would have to give way, not he, and you deserve better than that.' But these exhortations left Alma unmoved.

Some days later she was at the piano in her room working, when the chambermaid appeared and announced, portentously: 'Gustav Mahler is downstairs!' The Molls had recently moved into a charming house built and furnished by one of the architects of the Secession, Josef Hoffmann, in the Hohe Warte (Observatory) neighbourhood. There were velvet furnishings, oriental carpets on the walls, Japanese vases, beautiful *objets d'art* which Hoffmann came from time to time to deploy to best advantage. The Molls were also known to keep an excellent table.

But none of that interested Mahler. He came straight up to Alma's room, noticed some books still in piles on the floor waiting to be put on the shelves, examined them, made comments, waxed indignant at finding the works of Nietzsche, and advised Alma to throw them on the fire. Alma gave as good as she got. He grew impatient, and suggested they go for a walk. Going down the stairs he met Frau Moll who invited him to dinner that evening: 'There will be paprika chicken and Burckhard.' 'I don't like either', Mahler replied. But he accepted the invitation. He would just have to go down to the post office to telephone home.

Outside, the snow was crisp underfoot. Alma and Mahler set off at a round pace, but Mahler's shoe-laces kept coming undone. At the post office he realized he had forgotten his own telephone number, so he called the Opera to ask for it. He finally got through to his sister Justi and told her, without explanation, that he would not be home for dinner, something that hardly ever happened.

They went slowly back up the hill to the Hohe Warte as dusk fell on the shining snow, and Mahler finally delivered himself of his thoughts. 'It's not a simple matter', he said, 'to marry a man like me. I am entirely free and must remain so. I cannot tolerate any material worries. I could lose my job at the Opera from one day to the next . . .'.

This was a language Alma could understand. She knew how artists lived. On this point, at least, justice must be done to her: she respected creative work as something sacred. In her scale of values that came first. Before money, certainly, and before influence. They walked on for a long time in silence and arrived at the house. In Alma's room Mahler kissed her for the first time, and spoke of their getting married 'as if it was a simple, obvious thing, as if everything had been finally settled by the few words exchanged during the walk. So why wait?'

During the dinner Mahler was in fine form and charmed everyone with his conversation. Alma had let herself be kissed 'without really wanting to' and had allowed him to decide on their marriage. 'He alone can give a sense of direction to my life', she wrote. 'He stands head and shoulders above all the other men I have ever met.'

But Alma was not going to be as easy to win as that. Something in her resisted Mahler's authority, or any authority in fact. The next morning Mahler sent some of his Lieder round to her and she went through them with Zemlinsky, whose reaction was one of 'supreme disdain'. She herself found in them 'an affected simplicity and naïvety'. She felt they were 'not genuine'. But she said nothing of this to Mahler and, in her note thanking him for having sent the Lieder, she suggested that he should read what Maeterlinck had written about silence. 'It was very present in my mind', she wrote, 'during our first walk together.'

She kept her letter short, since her handwriting was execrable, something one had to get used to. Mahler never got used to it, and in the flood of correspondence they kept up with each other over the years, he regularly begged her to try and write more legibly. But behind the illegibility was something more serious. While Mahler was now relatively settled in his mind, Alma still had 'the feeling of belonging to Zemlinsky', whom she continued to see.

After a further visit by Mahler to the Hohe Warte, she wrote: 'He told me he loved me, we kissed, he played some of his music. My senses are silent . . . I must gradually put Alex out of my mind . . . I couldn't return his caresses. There was someone between us . . . If only we had met three years ago, my mouth still unprofaned!' The next day she wrote: 'I am in a terrible dilemma. I murmur softly "my beloved", then add at once "Alex". Can I love Mahler as much as he deserves? Shall I be able to do that? Shall I ever understand his art, and he mine?' Distressing doubts for a young bride-to-be.

She hesitated, questioned herself, thought over her feelings for the two men, and finally wrote:

I don't understand myself any more. I don't know if I love him or not, whether I love the director, the famous conductor, or the man . . . If I forget about the man, do I feel anything for the other and for his music which is so remote, so terribly remote from me? In a word, I don't believe in him as a composer. And if I have to link my life with that of a man . . . Really, he was nearer from afar than he is close to. I am afraid. We have kissed each other, but without holding each other close. He has expressive hands, but I don't like them as much as I do Alex's.

She remembered the fire those hands could kindle in the innermost recesses of her being. 'What am I to do? And what if Alex were to become famous and influential?' And finally she asked herself the question to which Mahler would soon give her an answer: 'One thing torments me. Will Mahler encourage me to work? Will he support my art? Will he like it in the same way as Alex likes it, for itself?'

Mahler saw her and wrote to her almost every day now, about all the things that it can occur to a man in love to write about. But then he left for Berlin, where Richard Strauss had included Mahler's Fourth Symphony in a series of concerts being given at the Opera. His departure brought Alma a certain relief. Zemlinsky or Mahler: this time her mind was made up, it was Mahler. 'I have the impression that he will make me a better being. He ennobles me. My desire for him will not weaken.'

But she was incorrigible. During Mahler's absence she received 'a handsome, rich, cultured, and musical' young man who had been courting her for some time. She played piano duets with him and then he asked her what her intentions were. She told him about Mahler, and he, 'pale and trembling', declared: 'If you refuse me, I shall put an end to my life.'

Before putting his threat into effect—which in fact he never did— he managed to pass on to Alma what a doctor friend of his had told him. Mahler was suffering from an incurable illness. Syphilis? Tuberculosis? Such words were left unspoken in those days. Incurable was enough. Moreover, there were clear signs that he was growing weaker. Alma's reaction was perfect. 'Oh God! I'll look after him like my own child. My youth and my strength will make him well again, my beloved master.'

Very revealing, too, are the things she wrote in her diary after having met Justi for the first time, again during Mahler's absence. The brother and sister were very close. Mahler had watched eight of his thirteen brothers and sisters die in their childhood. He was very attached to Justi, an affectionate little soul. From Berlin Mahler wrote to his sister: 'Please really get to like Alma, then I shall be even happier.' He asked her to help Alma learn how he lived and what kind of man he was.

The Zuckerkandls arranged for the two women to meet at their home. And, curiously, there were no sparks, indeed they liked each other and decided to meet again. Alma went to the Auenbruggergasse, where Justi showed her Mahler's room, his bed, his desk, his books, and proved to be 'very charming and sweet'.

Nevertheless, Alma was worried. 'I find it a strain to be constantly exposed to her searching, probing glances. That could be dangerous for me. What if it occurred to her, for example, that I was lacking in feeling and love—something I sometimes confess secretly to myself—that I am incapable of deep feelings, that everything in me is calculation, cold, clear calculation.'

'He is a sick man and his job can fold up from one day to the next. He is a Jew, his position is extremely precarious. Where then is the calculation?' The fact was that Alma's calculations, when she made any, were never of a humdrum kind. She couldn't have cared less about what others would have called her interests. But was she lacking, as she herself suspected, in feeling and love? She was indeed! She begrudged giving herself, this young woman who talked so often of 'giving'. That is why genuine happiness would always escape her, just when she thought she had achieved it, and why the sweets of the passions she aroused would leave her with a bitter taste. Deep down, she did not want to give. She wanted to receive love and fame, fame and love, as a tribute which the world owed to her.

So, while her fiancé was away she amused herself by driving to despair her handsome young, rich admirer, musician, and man of culture—and wrote about him to Mahler.

Then, at a performance of the *Meistersinger*, she noticed

the young Doctor Adler who pleases me and troubles me. I did rather more than flirt with him. We devoured each other with our eyes, while no one noticed. He has long, beautiful hands. There is an incredible voluptuousness in such glances, and he is incredibly handsome. His eyes are black as night—such a lovely face! He has breeding, and that's more than one can say of Mahler. Besides, I'm independent, faithful to Gustav in thought. Those bold glances don't come from the heart.

Quite.

She finally made up her mind to 'tell everything' to Zemlinsky. She wrote him a letter, in which, of course, she proposed that they should remain friends. And she noted in her diary: 'What a loss for me! This marvellous music teacher . . . '. A nice touch, that 'what a loss for me'! She was after all signing the death-warrant of a man who lived and breathed only for her.

Two days went by with no answer from Zemlinsky. And then he turned up again, of course. He could at least console himself with the thought that his rival was the only man in Vienna whom Alma and he had never disparaged, even though they were adepts at malicious gossip. Alma was impressed by Zemlinsky's calm demeanour, and was lavish in her praise of the 'manliness and magnanimity' he showed in agreeing to continue to teach her music. Poor Zemlinsky!

In Berlin Mahler was bored to death alone in his hotel, and wrote to Alma sometimes twice a day. He was a relentless correspondent, his letters splendid expositions of a man's point of view. For example:

I've caught myself (especially lately, since my thoughts have become bound up with you) entertaining a vulgar sort of ambition almost unworthy of someone like me! I now find myself wanting successes, recognition, and whatever else all these insignificant and, literally speaking, *meaningless* things are called! I'd like to be a credit to *you*! Don't misunderstand me when I talk of ambition! I've always had ambition, but not in the sense of the honours my neighbours and contemporaries can bestow on me. On the other hand, I've always striven to be understood and appreciated by my equals, even if I were not to meet them in my lifetime (and, indeed, they are only to be found beyond this time and space), and from now on that will be my highest aim in life. To achieve that, my beloved, *you* must help me. And, you know, to win this prize, this crown of laurels, one must forgo the acclaim of the crowd, nay, even that of the great and good (who also sometimes fail to understand). How gladly I've borne the slaps of the Philistines and the scorn and hatred of the ignorant [*Unmündigen*] up to now! Oh yes, I'm unfortunately all too well aware that the little respect I have won is perhaps due only to a misunderstanding, or at most an obscure presentiment of something higher but inaccessible. Needless to say, I'm not referring to my activities as a 'director' or a conductor, for these are, after all, and in the fullest sense of the words, only abilities and merits of a subordinate kind. I beg you to answer me on this question: do you understand what my path must be, and are you willing to follow me? Alma, could you endure with me all the rigours of adversity, the pointing fingers of scorn even, and cheerfully take up such a cross?

There he was explicitly demanding an answer. But in one of his subsequent letters comes this little passage: 'Please, Alma, don't forget to put in a word from time to time about the things I write in my letters to you. I want to know if you understand all I am saying and are willing to follow me . . . I should also like your answer to what I wrote in my last letter about ambition . . . '.

The same day he wrote a second letter in which he described the last rehearsal of the Fourth Symphony, which he was 'terribly pleased about'. 'I kept thinking all the time: if only my darling were down there in the audience. I would have been able to look so proudly at them! If it goes as well tomorrow, I shall really have made my mark in Berlin'. But it did not go well. There were boos and catcalls, and the music critics savaged the work and the composer. Berlin clearly did not love him.

And Alma, did she love him? Since he had left Vienna he had written six letters to her, each more elevated in tone than the last, and had received curious replies. One day she wrote that her letter would be shorter than usual because she was expecting Zemlinsky, who 'knew everything' and continued to give her lessons, 'thus surmounting his grief with great fortitude'. Another day she told him of her conversation with Burckhard when he had said that two people with personalities as strong as Alma's and Mahler's could never get on with each other. She also recounted the episode of the young suitor who had threatened to commit suicide. As always, the written words revealed what spoken words often failed to express. Mahler did not like what he read. He was astonished, shocked, and perturbed. Was there perhaps a basic misunderstanding between them as to the very meaning of their marriage?

Then, from Dresden, through which he was passing on his return from Berlin, he sent her twenty extraordinary pages which deserve to be quoted in full. They are unique in the history of love-letters.

19 December 1901

My dearest Almschi!
It's with a somewhat heavy heart that I'm writing to you today, my beloved Alma, for I know I must hurt you and yet I can't do otherwise. I've got to tell you the feelings that your letter of yesterday aroused in me, for they're so basic to our relationship that they must be clarified and thoroughly discussed once and for all if we're to be happy together.

Admittedly, I only read between the lines (for once again, my Almschi, it was only with the greatest difficulty that I managed to read the lines themselves). There seems to me to be a glaring contradiction between this letter and those which I've been receiving from you since the evening of *The Magic Flute*. You wrote then: 'I want to become the sort of person you *wish* and *need*! These words made me immensely happy and blissfully confident. Now, perhaps without realizing it, you take them back. Let me begin by going through your letter point by point.

First, your conversation with Burckhard: what do you understand by a personality [*Individualität*]? Do you consider yourself a personality? You remember I once told you that every human being has something indefinably personal that cannot be attributed to either heredity or environment. It's this that somehow makes a person peculiarly what he or she is and, in this sense, every human being is an individual [*Individuum*]. But what you and Burckhard mean is something quite different. A human being can only acquire the sort of personality you mean after a long experience of struggle and suffering and thanks to an inherent and powerfully developed disposition. Such a personality is very rare. Besides, you couldn't possibly already be the sort of person who's found a rational ground for her existence within herself and who, in all circumstances, maintains and develops her own individual and immutable nature and preserves it from all that's alien and negative, for everything in you is as yet unformed, unspoken, and undeveloped.

Although you're an adorable, infinitely adorable, and enchanting young girl with an upright soul and a richly talented, frank, and already self-assured person, you're still not a personality. What you are to me, Alma, what you could perhaps be or become—the dearest and most sublime object of my life, the loyal and courageous companion who understands and promotes me, my stronghold invulnerable to enemies from both within and without, my peace, my heaven in which I can constantly immerse myself, find myself again, and rebuild myself—is so unutterably exalted and beautiful, so much, and so great, in a word, my wife. But even this will not make you a personality in the sense in which the word is applied to those supreme beings who not only shape their own existence but also that of humanity and who alone deserve to be called personalities. I can tell you one thing, however, and that is that in order to be or to become such a personality, it's no use whatsoever just to desire or to wish it. Not one of the Burckhards, Zemlinskys, etc., is a *personality*. Each one of them has his own peculiarity, such as an eccentric address, illegible handwriting, etc. (I'm speaking figuratively, of course. It's not possible to reduce everything to such petty details.)

Now, after this somewhat lengthy introduction, I finally come to you. My

Alma, look! Your entire youth, and therefore your entire life, has been constantly threatened, escorted, directed (while you always thought you were independent), and abused by these highly confused companions who spend their time groping around in the dark and on false trails, drowning out their inner beings with loud shouting and continually mistaking the shell for the nut. They've constantly flattered you, not because you made a contribution of value to their lives but because you exchanged big-sounding words with them. (Genuine opposition makes them uncomfortable, for they only like grandiloquent words—I'm referring more to people like Burckhard than to Zemlinsky, whom I don't know but imagine to be rather better, although he too is undoubtedly confused and insecure. You intoxicated each other with verbosity (you think yourselves 'enlightened', but you merely drew your curtains so that you could worship your beloved gaslight as though it were the sun). Because you're beautiful and attractive to men, without realizing it they instinctively pay homage to your charm. Just imagine if you were ugly, my Alma. You've become (and however harsh I sound you'll nevertheless forgive me because of my real and already eternally inexhaustible love for you) vain about what these people think they see in you and wish to see in you (i.e. you would really like to be what you appear to them to be) but which, thank God, and as you yourself said in your sweet letter, is only the superficial part of you. For these people also flatter each other all the time and instinctively oppose a superior being because he disconcerts them and makes demands on them that they cannot live up to. But they find you, on account of your charms, an exceptionally attractive and, due to your lack of pertinent argument, a most *comfortable* opponent. Thus all of you have spent your time running around in circles and presuming to settle the affairs of humanity between you; when in fact you can't see further than your own noses.

There is an *arrogance* which is always characteristic of such people, who regard the insignificant and tortuous thought processes of their own exclusive circle as the only thing worthy of intellectual consideration. You too, my Almschi, are not entirely free from that. Some of your remarks (and I've no intention of taking you to task for them, for I know full well that they're only a manner of speaking—even though that, too, comes from an acquired way of thinking) such as that 'we don't *agree* on several things, ideas, etc.' prove it, as do many others! My little Alma, we must agree in *our* love and in our hearts—but in our ideas? My Alma, what are your ideas? Schopenhauer's chapter on women, the whole deceitful and viciously shameless immorality of Nietzsche's superiority of an élite, the turbid meanderings of Maeterlinck's drunken mind, Bierbaum and company's public house humour, etc., etc.? These, thank God, are not your ideas but theirs!

. . . So here I am, poor fellow, who couldn't sleep at night for joy at having found her, her who, *from the start*, was intimately at one with him in everything, who, as a woman, belonged wholly to him and had become an integral part of him; who had even written to him that she felt she could do nothing better than embrace and enter into his world; who, through her faith in him, no longer searches but has become convinced that his creed is hers, because she loves him, etc., etc. I must now ask myself again what this obsession is that has fixed itself in that little head I love so indescribably dearly, that you must be and remain yourself—and what will become of this obsession when once our passion is sated (and that will be very soon) and we have to begin, not merely residing, but living together and loving one another in companionship?

This brings me to the point that is the real heart and core of all my anxieties, fears, and misgivings, the real reason why every detail that points to it has acquired such significance: you write '*you* and *my* music—*forgive me, but there has to be a place for that too!*' In this matter, my Alma, it's absolutely imperative that we understand one another clearly *at once*, before we see each other again. I shall now have to start talking about myself, because I am, indeed, in the strange position of having, in a sense, to set *my* music against yours, of having to put it into the proper perspective and defend it against you, who don't really know it and in any case don't yet understand it. You won't think me vain, will you, Alma? Believe me, this is the first time in my life that I have discussed it with someone who doesn't have the right approach to it. Would it be possible for you, from now on, to regard *my* music as *yours*? I prefer not to discuss 'your' music in detail just now—I'll come back to it later. In general, however, how do you picture the married life of a husband and wife who are both composers? Have you any idea how ridiculous and, in time, how degrading for both of us such a peculiarly competitive relationship would inevitably become? What will happen if, just when you're 'in the mood', you're obliged to attend to the house or something I might happen to need, since, as you wrote, you want to spare me the menial details of life? Don't misunderstand me and start imagining that I hold the bourgeois view of the relationship between husband and wife, which regards the latter as a sort of plaything for her husband and, at the same time, as his housekeeper. Surely you would never suspect me of feeling and thinking that way, would you? But one thing is certain and that is that you must become 'what I need' if we are to be happy together: my wife, not my colleague. Would it mean the destruction of your life and would you feel you were having to forgo an indispensable highlight of your existence if you were to give up *your* music entirely in order to possess mine and also to be mine instead?

This point *must* be settled between us before we can even contemplate a union for life. For instance, what do you mean by 'I haven't done any work since . . . Now I'm going to get down to work', etc., etc. What sort of work? Composing? For your own pleasure or in order to enrich humanity's heritage?

He interrupted his letter to go and work, that is to say, to rehearse the Second Symphony. He had no choice, because 300 people were waiting for him, but in the afternoon he took up his pen again and went on, after a few words:

You have only *one* profession from now on: *to make me happy*! Do you understand what I mean, Alma? I'm quite aware that you must be happy with me in order to be able to make me happy, but the roles in this play, which could as easily turn out to be a comedy as a tragedy (and either would be wrong), must be correctly assigned. The role of 'composer', the 'worker's' role, falls to me, yours is that of the loving companion and understanding partner. Are you satisfied with it? I'm asking a great deal, a very great deal— and I can and may do so because I know what I have to give and will give in exchange.

I simply cannot understand the heartless way in which you treat Zemlinsky. Were you in love with him? Then how can you now demand that he play the unhappy role of continuing to be your teacher? You consider it manly and noble of him that, with suffering written on his face, he sits facing you, meek and silent and, as it were, 'obeys orders'? You were in love with him and can endure this? And what sort of a face should I put on if I were sitting there too—and you ought to be thinking of me as sitting there too! Is your life not subject to other forces of nature now? Hasn't its course been altered too much for you to be willing and able gradually to resume your former activities?

. . . What's all this about 'stubbornness', about 'pride'? Towards me who trustingly gave my whole heart and, from the first moment, dedicated my whole life to you (though I too know certain pretty, rich, cultivated, young, etc., girls and women). I beg you, Almschi, read my letter carefully. There must never be any question of a passing flirtation between us. Before we talk to each other again, things must be absolutely clear between us. You've got to know what I desire and expect from you, what I can offer you, and what you must be to me. You must 'renounce' (as you wrote) all superficiality, all convention, all vanity and delusion (as far as personality and work are concerned). You must give yourself to me unconditionally, shape your future life, in every detail, entirely in accordance with my needs and desire nothing in return save my *love*! What that love is, Alma, I can't tell you—I've talked of it too much already. I will say one thing more, however; I am prepared to sacrifice both my life and my happiness for the one I love as much as I would love you if you were to become my wife.

I had to unburden myself in this unrestrained and almost (it must seem immodest to you) immoderate manner today. And, Alma, I must have your answer to this letter before I come to see you on Saturday. I'll send a servant to pick it up.

A few more lines urged her to be 'ruthless' and say all she had to say. It would be better to separate at once than 'prolong a mistake'. His closing words were: 'Alma, I beseech you, be sincere.'

And that was it! The most astonishing letter a young woman of 22, until then spoilt by the gods, could receive. 'My citadel, my peace, my paradise, my wife': others before him have said it, others will say it until the end of time. But he admonishes her, suggesting that if her friends find her intelligent it is only because she is beautiful, vents his irony on her desire 'to be and to become herself', ridicules her literary and philosophical tastes in the tone of a man twenty years her senior who knows infinitely better. Finally, to crown it all, he purely and simply refuses to acknowledge her right to a separate existence, he takes her over, he absorbs her. Her music? What music?

At first Alma was speechless, overwhelmed, horrified. Then she showed the letter to her mother and discussed it with her late into the night. Anna Moll reacted sharply to the high-handed enslavement that Mahler was offering her daughter. You must finish with him, she said, break it off. But relations between mother and daughter were so ambivalent that the more Anna insisted, the more Alma was intoxicated by the heady perfume of sacrifice on the altar of genius.

The letter she handed the following morning to Mahler's servant for his master was purely and simply a capitulation. He had demanded: she promised. In the afternoon, back from Dresden, Mahler came to see her. He was happy. The clouds had dispersed. He brought her the score of the Fourth Symphony. She read it, and confessed artlessly: 'For that kind of thing, I prefer Haydn.' He laughed, convinced that one day she would change her mind. They played some of the work together at the piano . . .

After those happy hours together, Alma described at length the intensity of her feelings, and continued:

I feel that he uplifts me, whereas my association with Burckhard only aggravates my frivolity. I feel ashamed of my dirty jokes when Gustav is listening ... Is one happier with a frivolous, uncaring attitude to life, or when one has spun for oneself such a fine and lofty vision of the world? Freer in the first case, but happier? The loftier one's vision, the better one becomes. But doesn't that mean setting limits on freedom? Yes, yes, a thousand times yes! And, I can tell you, you'll have to be hard with yourself!

Their formal betrothal took place in the presence of the Molls and Justi on 23 December.

By one of the rare strokes of luck in Mahler's life, his sister, unbeknown to him, was having a love affair with the first violin of the Opera orchestra, Arnold Rosé, and wanted to marry him. Their marriage, which she had never dared to consider while it meant abandoning her brother, now became doubly convenient, since she could move out of the apartment in the Auenbruggergasse when Alma came to live there. There was general delight all round, in so far as Mahler's irritability permitted, and an atmosphere of suppressed excitement surrounded the wedding plans.

The engaged couple met often, did a lot of kissing and hugging, argued fiercely about Jesus and about Dostoevsky whom Mahler worshipped and Alma detested, of course. Nothing could have been more alien to her. Mahler was furious at Alma's Nietzschean indifference to all religious belief and 'found himself in the curious position of a Jew upholding Christ to a Christian'.

Mahler was a man of faith. Questioned later in the context of an enquiry on the subject of 'Why do you compose?', he gave the following splendid reply: 'Weaving the living garment of God, that at least is something . . . '. How different Alma was from him in this respect. And young, so young. He was uneasy: was she too young?

Someone was indiscreet, and the news that the director of the Opera was engaged to be married spread like wildfire through Vienna. The newspapers wrote at length of the youth, beauty, and musical talent of the woman who was going to marry the Maestro. Mahler became impatient, but Alma was not displeased with the letters, flowers, and telegrams of congratulation she received.

When she appeared for the first time at the Opera in the director's box, all eyes were upon her. Before and after the performance the audience applauded Mahler with particular warmth. That evening they were happy, and at Hartmann's restaurant where they went afterwards with the Molls and Justi and Rosé, they fixed the date for the wedding ceremony.

In the mean time, however, Alma witnessed a scene which left her thunderstruck. At Mahler's invitation, Richard Strauss came to conduct his second opera, *Feuersnot*, at the *Hofoper*. Strauss was the most well-known of Mahler's contemporaries in the world of music. He was also the anti-Mahler incarnate, a fair-haired giant, easygoing, someone who enjoyed living a life which had been roses, roses all the way. Admired and fêted since the age of 12, in Germany they called him 'Richard II'. Acknowledged to be a superb conductor, Richard II was also very interested in making money.

Much less demanding than Mahler, whose 'frightful nervousness' always surprised him, he was profoundly impressed by the quality of the Vienna orchestra—which was probably the best in Europe—and very satisfied with the performance he had conducted. But then there was Frau Strauss, the singer Pauline de Ahna, a kind of volcanic tigress whose unpredictable explosions had made her famous.

On the evening of the first performance of *Feuersnot*, sitting in the director's box beside Alma, she grumbled: 'What filthy rubbish! It's impossible to like that. Mahler made a mistake, pretending to find it good . . . He must know that it's all been stolen from Wagner, Maxi, and others!' 'Who is Maxi?' Alma asked. 'An infinitely better composer than Strauss', said Pauline, 'Max von Schillings'.

Strauss was called back ten times to acknowledge the applause. There were a few catcalls too. They all met offstage, and Strauss asked his wife what she thought of the concert. She 'leapt at his throat like a wild cat' and roared: 'You thieving hound! How can you look me in the face! You disgust me!' Embarrassed, Mahler ushered the Strauss couple into a rehearsal room and waited outside to take them to supper when they had finished quarrelling. The raised voices went on and on. Tired of waiting, Mahler announced that he was going on ahead, with Alma, to the restaurant. The door flew open, and Strauss appeared while Pauline was shouting: 'You can go. I'm going home to bed, and tonight I'll sleep alone.'

'I'll come with you as far as the hotel', suggested Strauss timidly. 'Alright. But you'll walk ten paces behind me!' said Pauline. Which he did.

At the restaurant, where he finally rejoined Alma and Mahler, he excused his wife's behaviour: 'She's got a rough tongue, but it's something I need.' The conversation then turned to the problems of authors' rights, with Strauss jotting down calculations in pencil. Yes, that was Richard Strauss: a masochistic genius-cum-commercial traveller!

The strange evening at least enabled Mahler and Alma to feel united in agreement as to the impression it had made on them. 'I am very proud that you so quickly perceived the truth', Mahler said to her. 'Isn't it better to eat the bread of poverty and walk in the light than sell one's soul for vulgar profit!'

But such agreement was rare. They often differed and quarrelled, and then Mahler at once adopted his attitude of mentor. Nevertheless, 'it seems that they are both very much in love', wrote Bruno Walter to his parents.

Alma noted that Mahler had confided to her that he was sexually inexperienced and that this caused him some anxiety—anxiety which she just could not understand, she wrote. According to her diary, she decided to give herself to him without more delay, out of regard 'for his physical and mental health'. From which we perceive that she had her own ideas about hygiene.

The day came when the engaged couple 'were almost united' in the room in which he received her. Mahler was 'agitated and worried', but she experienced 'a pure and holy feeling', while at the same time fearing 'that a feeling of shame and sin might spoil the magnificent and holy mystery'.

She wrote: 'We could hardly tear ourselves away from one another. Why these terrible conventions? Why can't I simply draw him close to me? Our desire consumes us and consumes the best of our strength. He bares his chest and I put my hand on his heart. I feel that his body belongs to me . . . '.

She let down her hair because he liked to see the strands float free. 'To have a child by him! His mind, my looks! To be wholly his!' Two days later they were together again in the same room in the Auenbruggergasse and exchanged caresses. Then came the fiasco. He 'lay powerless . . . weeping almost for shame . . . dejected, distressed'.

And she wrote: 'I can't say how much all that irritated me. First the growing agitation deep within me, the approach to the goal . . . and the failure to reach it! And then his self-torturings, his incredible self-torturings! My beloved!'

Three days later, again in her diary, three words—'Bliss upon bliss' (*Wonne über wonne*)—seem to indicate that Mahler had triumphed over himself. But a few days later, she noted: 'My poor Gustav is having medical treatment. Inflammation, swelling, ice-bag, hip-baths, etc. Is it because of my having resisted so long? How he must be suffering!' From which it would appear that Mahler's trouble was due less to lack of experience than to haemorrhoids, which have never been known to act as an erotic stimulant! And that the lack of experience was rather on Alma's side.

Their intimate love-life as a married couple remains a mystery. After Mahler's death Alma put it about that he was more or less impotent, that he never or hardly ever touched her—and then so clumsily. He was a frail puritan for whom pleasure and guilt always went hand in hand, according to her. That he was impotent is hardly likely. Others who had had affairs with him would not have hesitated to make it known. A childhood memory, which he told Alma about, seems to have marked him.

He was 11 years old, staying as a boarder in Prague with a family, the Grünfelds, when he came by accident on the son of the house lying on top of the maidservant, who was moaning and crying. He wanted to help her, but their main concern was that he should not tell anyone. From this scene he had concluded: that is what my mother must have suffered, those are the pains, the violence, she had to endure. He may well then have resolved that he neither could nor would ever inflict similar suffering. Certainly the scene always remained in his memory and must in some way have determined certain aspects of his behaviour.

According to the psychoanalyst Theodor Reik, Mahler was obsessed by the image of the Virgin Mary as a representative figure of the feminine ideal which raises man to higher things. It was this idealization, this sublimated concept of woman, which inhibited his sexual approaches to his own wife.

The Mahlers always slept in separate rooms, as was customary among the bourgeoisie of the time. According to an immutable ritual, he did not join Alma in bed until she was asleep. Whatever his morbid fantasies, his fears, or his inhibitions may have been, it certainly seems likely that Mahler was less skilled as a lover than as a conductor, and that from that point of view, too, Alma was frustrated. She evidently expected from a man something other than clumsy and furtive embraces—especially from a man who claimed that he would enslave her, never mind the fine names Mahler found to describe such enslavement. And this fuelled the resentment she would one day hold against him.

But that day was still to come. For the present she was 22 years old, she admired her fiancé, she discovered she was pregnant, which was a 'source of much torment' and painful attacks of sickness which had at all costs to be concealed, and she was about to become acquainted with some of her future husband's friends and cronies. Even if they had all belonged to the cream of the most precious élite in her world, Alma would have turned up her nose at them. We have already mentioned her pathological jealousy of anyone else who was the object of affection past or present. However, Mahler's friends were quite simply his friends, people without any particular claim to fame.

His own family origins were modest. He came from Iglau, a small town in Bohemia in which his father, after much effort, had succeeded in becoming proprietor of a distillery. A hard and humourless man, the father nevertheless recognized his son's outstanding talent as a pianist, and did all he could to help him in his musical and university studies. He sent him to study in Vienna, where the young man's career took off. But Mahler was burdened all his life with the memory of a childhood of poverty and misfortune, of a family in which eight of his brothers and sisters had died young, of a sorrowing mother overwhelmed with work. He supported two of his brothers who were incapable of shifting for themselves.

One day he said to Alma: 'You're lucky. You come from a brilliant, successful family. You can trip lightly through life, unencumbered by painful memories and a family that depends on you. For me, life has always been hard. I've got mud on my boots.

It was not simply personal dislike which prevented him from frequenting refined, carefree Viennese society—he was opposed to it on principle. Apart from very rare exceptions, like the Zuckerkandls, he sought his friends elsewhere. For their part, Mahler's habitual friends were full of prejudice against Alma. She suspected them all of being narrow-minded, petty bourgeois whom Mahler 'had been dragging behind him since his childhood like cannon-balls chained to his feet'. They suspected her of being too beautiful, too brilliant, too free in her manners, language, and clothes to be a suitable companion for Mahler.

Six weeks before the wedding the happy fiancé organized a dinner at his home so that the two sides could meet. There was the writer Siegfried Lipiner, and his wife. Lipiner had had brilliant early successes as a disciple of Nietzsche, but had not achieved much since. He was Mahler's favourite intellectual sparring partner. There was Lipiner's previous wife, Nana, and her husband Albert Spiegler, a friend of Mahler's since their 'teens. There was Anna von Mildenburg, the singer with whom he had formerly had an affair. And there were the Molls, Justi, Rosé, and Kolo Moser, a young painter-decorator, member of the Secession, and friend of the Molls.

Alma behaved impossibly. Her rare contributions to the general conversation were either rude or tactless. She declared that she had 'had a good laugh' at Plato's *Symposium*. She told Mildenburg, who had asked her about Mahler's music: 'I know very little of it, and the little I do know I don't like.'

General consternation! Could it be that Mahler had found his Pauline and that, like Strauss, he found it good for him? No, their relationship was not like that, either then or later. But that evening he was in love. So he laughed, found an excuse to persuade Alma to come to his room, and shut the door so that he might kiss her undisturbed. When an embarrassed Justi came at last to look for them, the dinner had turned into a disaster. The Lipiners and the Spieglers had had enough, and more than enough. It took years for Mahler to become good friends with them again.

In the mean time, he received a fierce letter from Lipiner reproaching him for his 'profound and everlasting coldness', his egotism. 'At heart,' he continued, 'you don't consider us as persons, we're all just objects to you.'

As for Alma, Lipiner considered that her behaviour showed her to be 'vain, superficial, lacking in warmth, devoid of naturalness, sincerity, and good sense'. Her conversation showed her to be a 'spiteful, vain, overbearing' person. And, he wondered, what meaningful bond could there be between Mahler and such a person?

One may indeed wonder why Alma, so ready to exercise her charm on man or woman when she wanted to, had behaved in this way. Whatever her motive, she had made a thorough job of it: Mahler's old friends left him. It was time to have done with this strange pre-nuptial interim during which he ceaselessly tormented himself because of the difference in their ages and, indeed, the more fundamental differences in their characters which emerged so clearly in all their conversations, while she felt more and more under constraint.

'Things are no longer what they were', she wrote.

He wants me to be different, totally different. I can manage it when I am with him, but when I am alone my second self, vain and wicked, returns, insists on expressing itself, and I must give way to it. Frivolity gleams in my eyes, my mouth keeps telling lies. And he feels it, knows it. I've only just this moment realized it. I must go to him.

She would raise herself up to his level: that, clearly, was the illusion that kept her going. Even if she despised his music, she had sensed the stature, the moral strength, of Mahler, whose tyranny was only a form of his thirst for the absolute. In this respect Alma's choice—and we have seen that she did not lack for suitors—had something fine about it and reflected the best in her, namely an infallible sense of quality, in men as in things. But at the same time she wrote: 'I must start at once the struggle to win and defend my rightful place. I mean artistically. The fact is that he thinks nothing of my art and much of his, while I think nothing of his and much of mine. That's how it is.'

That was indeed how the battle lines were drawn for her. As for him, it may well be that, in spite of the suffering she caused him, this glittering creature so little suited to the role he had assigned to her was the catalyst he needed to give meaning to his life, his struggle, his work.

5. 'A Semblance of a Life'

The wedding took place on 9 March 1902 in the strictest privacy: the bride and bridegroom and the witnesses (the Molls and the Rosés). To avoid all publicity, the ceremony was held in the vestry of the Karlskirche. Nevertheless, the journalist Karl Kraus, seizing the occasion to vent his spite on Mahler, whom he detested, commented drily on the 'pretended privacy', the presence of the press, and 'a distinguished crowd'.

Leaving the Mahlers for a moment, safely married and comfortably installed on the train that was taking them to Russia, let us say something more about Karl Kraus, since he will crop up again several times in our story. He certainly had a venomous tongue but, more than that, he was an intellectual terrorist who held all Vienna in thrall. He had tried, unsuccessfully, to be an actor, and then taken up journalism. In 1899 he had founded a review, *Die Fackel* (The Torch), which appeared between red covers at irregular intervals. The review had 10,000 subscribers who devoured each issue as eagerly as if it were a contemporary version of the Bible. In its pages, Karl Kraus attacked, bit, savaged, denigrated, denounced, launched crusades against all forms of scandal: a slipshod treaty, bribes, illegal favours, embezzlement.

He often got into trouble, was taken to court, or physically assaulted. He had a violent dispute with Moll after reporting information he had wormed out of Alma during a dinner, something about an exhibition. Some days later, sitting in the Café Imperial with her stepfather, Alma caught sight of Kraus, and pointed him out to Moll. 'It's that dirty dog, is it!' said Moll, and got to his feet. But Kraus had fled. On another occasion Alma attended with delight a libel action which went against Kraus.

Yet such affairs revealed only the more ordinary, run-of-the-mill side of the man and his activity. The corruption he denounced most severely—and in this he was highly original—was corruption of language. His criticism of words, their misuse, and the resulting corruption of minds, was authoritative and all-embracing. A 'Daumier of language', he preached not just a set of rules but a philosophy of purity. According to him, only a return to the language of Goethe could cleanse political life of its equivocation.

This led him to adopt a similar position on art, which he felt should be stripped of all the affectations with which the Secessionists had cluttered it. In music he had ears only for the atonal Schönberg. In painting, his choice was Kokoschka. In architecture he rooted for Adolf Loos. Viennese aestheticism seemed to him to be a romantic flight into illusion. He wanted purity, sobriety, and rigour. Later in the course of his career he also denounced the class character of the works of the younger generation of Viennese writers (Arthur Schnitzler, Hermann Bahr, Hugo von Hofmannsthal, Peter Altenberg), their obsession with form, and indifference to social problems.

A self-appointed judge, Karl Kraus delivered his verdicts, and even those he offended could not refrain from reading him. He was the king of Vienna. And his reign was to be a long one since, after a voluntary interruption during the First World War when he wrote a twelve-hour play consisting of extracts from newspapers, *Die Fackel* resumed publication and continued until his death in 1936. But he was to finish without an audience, shorn of his glory and influence, indeed finally discredited. The old unruly social democratic contro-versialist, who kept so many audiences spellbound with his lectures on purity and intransigence, could think of nothing more to say about Hitler than: 'As for Hitler, I have nothing to say.' The king lost his crown before he died.

His list of favourite targets included Freud, to whom he turned a deaf ear ('psychoanalysis is the mental illness of which it claims to be the remedy'); Berta Zuckerkandl, whom he nicknamed 'the cultural midwife'; and Mahler, although in his case he was prepared to recognize some qualities. He slaughtered the first performance of the Second Symphony, at which incidentally he was not present. In the autumn of 1901 he launched a virulent attack against Mahler's management of the *Hofoper*: 'Up to now the liberal press has passed in silence over Herr Mahler's shameful exploitation of the artistic resources of the house, the unimaginable decadence of the repertory', and so on. Karl Kraus was a master of the short, pithy maxim. Here is just one example: 'We don't even live once.'

But it is time for us to rejoin the Mahlers, now returned from their honeymoon trip to St Petersburg, which they had much enjoyed, it seems. Mahler had given three concerts which had been much applauded and handsomely remunerated. They had been received everywhere with great hospitality: the Duke of Mecklenburg, a member of the Imperial family, had invited them to dinner. True, Mahler had had one of those terrible migraines which sometimes plagued him, and of course he had caught a cold (as she had too) after going for a ride in an open troika. But Alma was relieved not to have to conceal her pregnancy any longer, and Mahler's letters to Justi show him in a relaxed mood.

So now they were at home, in the Auenbruggergasse, Justi having moved out. The neighbouring apartment had been vacated by its tenant and combined with theirs. They now had six rooms in all. What they were short of was not comfort, but money. Mahler earned a good salary, but had got into debt when he had had the house built at Maiernigg in which he worked during his holidays. He had even borrowed from the portion of his parents' legacy reserved to provide dowries for his sisters, and Justi, not gifted in domestic management, had never been able to adjust her brother's life-style to his financial position.

Alma took things in hand. Nothing had prepared her for this kind of problem, since she had always lived in carefree luxury, but she was a born organizer. What was more, she considered it her job to preserve Mahler from trivial concerns. She drew up a household budget, and a plan for paying the debt off in instalments over five years.

Did she really have to go without as much as she said she did on many occasions? There was the visit to the Baron of Rothschild which she had to turn down for lack of a hat to wear. The same dresses were worn again and again, although she liked to dress well and had excellent taste, whereas Mahler bought his footwear from the best English shoemaker. Let us say that she had to do her sums carefully—for both of them, since he refused to worry about such things.

Their daily life was as precisely regulated as a clock. He got up at 7 a.m. and installed himself at his worktable, took his breakfast there, and left for the Opera at 8.45. Shortly before 1 p.m. there would be a call from his office to say that he was leaving. A quarter of an hour later a ring at the main door downstairs would warn the cook to prepare to serve the soup while he was climbing the stairs to the fourth floor. When he got home he would walk through all the rooms of the apartment slamming the doors behind him, wash his hands in the bathroom, and burst into the dining-room where Alma was waiting for him.

After a brief post-prandial siesta, Alma, pregnant or not, would have to accompany him on their walk—either a turn around the Belvedere park or the complete circuit of the Ring. Sometimes she dared to refuse. At 5 p.m. they had tea at home, after which he went off again to the Opera where, even when he was not conducting, he always stayed for part of the performance.

In the evening she came to fetch him. If he had not finished his work he would send her to sit in the director's box. There were operas whose endings she never knew, since he would come to fetch her at a time which suited him. They would go home on foot, and dine. After dinner, he would sometimes ask her to read aloud to him. That was Alma Mahler's life.

She occasionally saw the Molls, the Rosés, the Zuckerkandls, or Kolo Moser who had designed audacious pregnancy gowns for her. When, during a heatwave, she accompanied Mahler to Krefeld where the first performance of the Third Symphony was to be given as part of the Festival of Contemporary Music, her appearance caused a sensation in the street.

The journey from Vienna to Krefeld had been painful. Since there was no suitable hotel the Mahlers stayed with one of the inhabitants, a wealthy silk merchant who received them with mistrust. The family regarded Mahler as 'a famous theatre director who had composed for his pleasure a monstrous symphony' which he wished to inflict on others. One day Mahler came out of his room and accidentally kicked over a bucket of water which clattered down the stairs and came to rest at the feet of the lady of the house. Disgusted, she exclaimed: 'Really, Herr Mahler, the Graces were certainly not standing over your cradle.'

He received a visit in his room from a neo-romantic German composer, Hans Pfitzner, who was there for the Festival and profited from the occasion to come and make a request: would Mahler put on his latest work, *Die Rose vom Liebesgarten*, in Vienna? Before receiving the young man, Mahler had hidden Alma in the alcove, behind a curtain. He greeted Pfitzner coldly. He would not put on *Die Rose*, as it was too long and the libretto was not clear. Pfitzner pleaded his case but Mahler stood firm. Pfitzner was about to leave, disappointed, when Alma suddenly emerged from her hiding-place and warmly shook him by the hand. She ultimately persuaded Mahler to put on *Die Rose*, three years later.

Krefeld was swarming with critics, composers, conductors, all there to take part in the Festival. Wonder of wonders! For the first time in his career as a composer Mahler got a triumphant reception. The Third Symphony, a monumental work which had had to wait six years for its first performance, was understood, hailed, applauded beyond anything Mahler had ever experienced as a composer. There is no evidence to indicate how Alma reacted to this triumph, or whether her opinion of her husband's music was in the slightest degree modified by it.

In fact, she would never acknowledge his true stature for a reason which appears again and again in her writings: Burckhard had put the idea into her head that Jews were incapable of creative work. Alma's anti-Semitism was rather special, since two of her husbands were Jews. But she seemed to be subject to sporadic bouts of it. This intelligent woman would then write things like: 'Jews don't like flowers!', 'Jews, like all mediocre people, love Italian music.' And one wonders what use her intelligence was to her. She also wrote: 'I could not live without Jews . . .', and one is almost afraid to guess why. The Jews being in some undefined way 'inferior', she felt deliciously superior when she was with them, endowed as she was with what she called her 'Christian splendour'.

Krefeld marked a turning point in Mahler's career. From then on every German city wanted a performance of the Third Symphony.

Music publishers too began to change their attitude. He was a happy man, therefore, when he left with Alma for Maiernigg, where they would spend their summer holidays, the period Mahler reserved for composing. The house at Maiernigg, on the Wörthersee between the lake and the woods, is still standing. It is a sturdy, inelegant, two-floored chalet, perched on a steeply sloping plot of land.

Alma found it newly built and furnished by Justi. It was roomy, with five or six main rooms looking out over the lake, surrounded by a garden and a patch of woodland. The view was beautiful, the interior ugly. Alma began by removing the little columns supporting the cornices of the cupboards. Near the house, in the woods, Mahler had had a bungalow built (his 'Häuschen') which housed a piano and a few books. That was where he worked.

That summer he finished the Fifth Symphony. He rose every morning at 6 a.m., and rang for the cook, Elise, to carry his breakfast at once to the Häuschen. Since he did not wish to see anyone before starting to work, Elise had to take a steep little path that kept her out of Mahler's sight. As soon as he was ensconced, there had to be absolute silence. Alma saw to it, and persuaded the nearest neighbours to keep their dogs indoors.

Shortly after midday, he stopped working and went down to the lake for a swim. He was a good swimmer and did not mind the chilly lake water. He had had a little boathouse built, with a bathing cabin on each side from which steps led straight down into the water. The roof was flat, providing a platform for sunbathing.

Once in the water, he would whistle for Alma to come and join him. After the swim, he would sunbathe, while Alma, no doubt, put something on. Suntan was hardly fashionable in those days. Then both of them would go back up to the house through the garden, Mahler stopping to admire every plant. Alma had no eye for that sort of thing.

As soon as they reached the house, lunch had to be on the table. He could only stand light, mildly flavoured, thoroughly cooked dishes, which annoyed Alma, accustomed as she was to a more sophisticated cuisine and convinced that these insipid meals 'were bad for the stomach'.

After a brief siesta they set out on one of his interminable walks, Mahler taking the lead in short, unpredictable bursts, it being taken for granted that she accompanied him. If she lagged behind—she was five months pregnant—he would stop, murmur 'I love you', and set off again. Heartened by this encouragement, she had to carry on too. Or, on the other hand, she might have to halt without a word because he had taken a notebook from his pocket and was jotting down a musical idea, beating out the rhythm with his pencil. And it sometimes took a long time. She waited.

Sometimes they walked along by the side of the lake, sometimes crossed by boat to the other side. They took no notice of the well-dressed holiday-makers who habitually clustered round the jetty at Unterach when boats were due to arrive.

In short, Alma spent her time either walking or being on her own, sometimes for eight hours a day. It is not surprising that we find her writing, in mid-July:

I don't know what to do. My mind is torn with conflicting impulses. Left to suffer on my own, I long to find someone who would think of me, help me to find myself. I am no more than a housewife.

I sit down at the piano, dying to play, but musical notation no longer means anything to me. My eyes have forgotten how to read it. I have been firmly taken by the arm and led away from myself. And I long to return to where I was. I have lost all my friends for the sake of one who does not understand me!

That same summer she complained to her husband. Mahler, 'in his infinite goodness', wondered how he could help her. She was appeased by that. But a whole day alone reduced her to tears again and she wrote:

When I'm in a loving mood I can put up with everything very easily. When I'm not, things become impossible! If only I could recover my inner equilibrium. I don't want him to notice the struggles I am having. He told me yesterday that he had never worked so long and so easily as now, and that delighted me. But . . . I have never cried so much as I do now, and yet I have everything a woman can wish for.

Completely absorbed in his work, did Mahler take Alma's distress seriously? He was certainly aware of it, and one day composed with her in mind a short, tender Lied, 'Liebst du um Schönheit'. He slipped the manuscript of it between the pages of the *Siegfried* score she had left lying on the piano, so that she might find it there.

But days passed, and she still hadn't opened the score. Unable to bear it any longer, he handed the book to her, and the sheet fell to the floor. It was 'the first song of love, a tender secret between us', written for her alone, and the offering overwhelmed her. Thus ended, in 'splendid isolation', those summer months in which Alma's mood vacillated between the deepest melancholy and moments of exaltation when she felt herself transported by Mahler to the highest peaks.

The holidays over, Mahler completed the Fifth Symphony in Vienna, and dedicated it to her: 'To my dearest Almschi, my courageous and faithful companion.' In Vienna Alma was subject to the same strict timetables. But there, at least, she had the Molls and the rare friend or two whom Mahler could put up with. The baby was becoming due. The doctor had forecast a difficult birth; they were careful not to say anything to Mahler. On 3 November 1902, while Alma was dying a thousand deaths on her bed of suffering, he paced ceaselessly up and down through all the rooms of the apartment. The labour was interminable. Finally, she gave birth to a little girl. There was intense relief, joy, emotional scenes. 'Things were difficult', the doctor told Mahler, 'because the baby presented itself bottom first.' Mahler roared with laughter, and exclaimed: 'That's my child! She shows the world straight away what she thinks of it: her bottom!' In memory of Mahler's mother they christened the child Maria, and nicknamed her Putzi.

The happy father fell in love with her immediately. When she was ill, he would spend hours rocking her tenderly in his arms, murmuring sweet nothings in her ear, as if he knew by instinct how to talk to babies. Alma's instinct was less sure—indeed, it was non-existent. Putzi caused no maternal chord to vibrate in her, provided her with no 'reason for living' which would have enabled her to throw off her unhappiness.

Five weeks after her baby's birth she wrote, with her usual confused imagery, these sad lines:

I often feel as if my wings have been clipped. Gustav, why did you bind to yourself this magnificent bird, so eager to soar, when another, heavy and dull, would have suited you better . . . I have been ill for a long time. Gallstones. Cause or consequence perhaps of my secret worries. But for several days and nights I have been weaving music in my mind. So loud and

so persistent that I can feel it behind the words I speak, and cannot get to sleep at night . . .
      Gustav lives his life, and I too must live his life. My child doesn't need me. In any case I can't keep myself busy solely with *that*.
      I am learning Greek. But my God, what has happened to my ambition, my splendid ambition? May God help me!

Her mood hardened, became spiteful. She made a ridiculous jealous scene over two singers, 'that Mildenburg woman and that Weidt woman', pushed her husband away when he approached her, saying: 'You disgust me!', then repented, and wrote: 'When I am unhappy it's not his fault, but mine alone.'

Her diary, a dreary catalogue of complaints mingled with self-accusations, for several months contains only expressions of torment and regret. What had happened to the lovely, the brilliant, the glorious Alma? It was as if the music she was continually regurgitating and unable to express, her music, was acting like a poison. There were no physical symptoms, but her self-confidence, her capacity to enjoy life had disappeared.

During this period, the thing she did best, with the help of the chambermaid Poldi, was packing Mahler's bags for his frequent journeys. He had to be able to put his hand immediately on the aspirin when he had an attack of migraine. As mistress of the house, the energetic organizer of their daily lives, she was beyond reproach. And, of course, it never occurred to Mahler to be grateful to her for that. Wasn't it quite natural? Does one ever notice when a house is well-run? It is only when something goes wrong that one becomes aware of it and that never happened with Alma.

In April 1903 her spirits were revived somewhat by the arrival in Vienna of Gustave Charpentier, composer of the opera *Louise*, which Mahler was putting on, and a short visit by Richard Strauss who had come to conduct two concerts.

The Frenchman was a character. He wandered around in a black cape, spat on the table, bit his nails. But Alma was attracted by 'his lightheartedness, the way he had of not taking himself seriously, his Bohemian lack of constraint and his exaggerated gallantry'. When he squeezed her knee in her box at the Opera, she found it charming. Every day he sent her flowers, with a card bearing the words: 'To Madame Mahler, gracious Muse of Vienna, with thanks from the

Muse of Montmartre.' He courted her, told her the story of his life, tried, unsuccessfully, to get her to share his socialist convictions, and told Mahler: 'How lucky you are to have such a lively girl about you! She's all lightness and fun, the springtime all artists have need of.' Sweet summer rain on Alma's bitter heart.

The Strausses came to dine at the Auenbruggergasse. Strauss was mainly concerned with setting up an association of authors, and wanted Mahler to become a member. During the evening Pauline, as usual, behaved impossibly, to the extent that Strauss finally took Mahler into the neighbouring room so that they could talk seriously. Pauline then enumerated her complaints against Strauss. He never spoke to her, never gave her enough money, when he had finished working he went out to play cards. Ah! how hard it was to live with a genius! And she burst into tears. Alma went to fetch the two husbands. What were they talking about? Mommsen's *History of Rome*, on which they did not agree. She brought them back to the drawing-room, where the conversation took a surrealist turn, reflections on Beethoven interspersed with interruptions by Pauline who wanted details about the best hairdressers in Vienna and the best shops for underwear.

Pauline was a formidable person. One day Alma paid her a visit and was surprised to find her in bed. Strauss arrived with a diamond ring which he held out to his wife, saying: 'Now will you agree to get up!' During the evening they spent at the Auenbruggergasse she probably horrified Alma by providing her with what amounted to a caricature of herself in the role of the oppressed wife of a genius. Nevertheless, the Strausses made a change.

During the season, Mahler was often away. Since the Krefeld triumph he no longer had to canvass for engagements, and he could insist that one of his works be included in the programme when he agreed to conduct a concert, and for a fee which was now considerably higher.

Whenever he was away, he wrote to his wife every day. But what curious letters to a young anguished wife who was trying to express in her own letters what she could no longer bring herself to tell him when they were together. For example:

Lemberg, 2 April 1903

It seems that my example has not taught you very much. What use to you are Paulsen [a German philosopher] and all the other prophets if you get lost over and over again in irrelevancies? Independence is just an empty word if one does not possess inner freedom. But that one can only achieve by oneself. Do me a favour, therefore, and think how you can improve yourself . . .

And a few days later:

One must always make the best of everything and whenever one is feeling depressed think of the real suffering in the world. If I didn't do that myself, I should spend my days weeping and groaning, and would come back home skin and bones. It's certainly no fun for me to travel all over the place to earn a few pence without knowing that there is one place at least where I can get some comfort . . .

Mahler had no idea how to cope with his wife's moods, which, obviously, he simply could not understand. After all, he loved her. What more could she want?

That summer, at Maiernigg, while he was composing the first movement of the Sixth Symphony, he said one morning after coming back down from the Häuschen: 'I have tried to portray you in one of the themes. I don't know if I have succeeded, but I think you will like it!'

According to Henry-Louis de La Grange, she appears 'in the form of an ascending theme in F major, impetuous and determined, which brings to this first movement a brief moment of health and optimism'. But the role of provider of inspiration did nothing to relieve her profound depression. And she had still not ventured to start composing again.

She had nightmares. This one, for example: 'A large green long-legged reptile forced its way deep inside me. I caught it by the tail and pulled. It would not move. I rang for the maid. She, too, pulled with all her strength. It had all my internal organs in its jaws. I was left empty and hollow like the broken carcase of a ship.' No doubt about it, Alma was in a bad way. If only she had gone to Doctor Freud and told him all about it! But Mahler was the one who would go to him— later, when he was speechless with anguish.

Meanwhile, she was pregnant again. Mahler left without her, for Amsterdam and the Rhineland. And she rebelled.

I must begin another life, I can't stand this one any more. My discontent increases hour by hour. I am just vegetating. I must start reading again, learn something.

I must take piano lessons again. I must have an inner intellectual life, as I used to! What a misfortune to have no friends any more, but Gustav doesn't want to see anyone.
How full my life was once, how empty now! I need stimulating. If only Pfitzner lived in Vienna! If only I had the right to see Zemlinsky! Schönberg interests me too. I have thought it over. Things must change!

And things did change, to some extent. Zemlinsky and Schönberg decided to form a music group modelled on the Secession, a lofty ambition for which they required the moral and financial support of their elders.

The two of them came to see Mahler, who finally agreed to become honorary president of their association. The important thing was that the ban on Zemlinsky was lifted. The two young composers became constant visitors at the Auenbruggergasse. The circle of loneliness was broken.

Alma also took up again with Burckhard, and asked him to organize some dinners with literary personalities. Had Mahler understood that he could not continue to confine his wife to the lonely role he had hitherto imposed on her? He agreed to the idea. The reunions occasionally went wrong, when they invited Hermann Bahr, for example, one of the rowdiest of Vienna's intellectuals. Mahler then emanated 'an atmosphere of unbearable embarrassment, a kind of oppression'. But it was at the Burckhards that the Mahlers met the best known of the German playwrights, Gerhard Hauptmann (*The Weavers*) and his wife, with whom they became friends.

Alma was enjoying a little more freedom therefore when, in June, returning from the theatre where they had been to see a play by Hauptmann, she felt the first labour pains. She called her husband to tell him to summon the midwife, and he took it upon himself to help her bear the pains. How? By reading aloud to her from a book by Kant.

Alma's patience in regard to her celebrated husband's odd behaviour was remarkable. She did not hold it against him, even though she was sometimes ashamed of the consequences his absent-mindedness or other peculiarities could have. Obviously in her eyes these strange ways were part and parcel of Mahler's greatness, of the creative side of him which she respected.

What she could not stand were the privations he imposed on her:

no work of her own to accomplish, no man to charm, nothing on which to exercise her ability, a void. That night, however, Kant got on her nerves and she begged her husband to let her suffer in peace. At midday the following day she gave birth to a little girl, whom they christened Anna after Anna Moll. That same evening the young mother was dozing peacefully when she awoke with a start: an enormous cockchafer was hovering beside her face. Mahler was dangling it by one leg. 'I know you adore animals,' he said, 'so I caught this one for you!'

Fortunately, he went off to work at Maiernigg, leaving Alma in Vienna. She was under orders to keep to her bed for three weeks. One can imagine that she was thankful to be left alone. Some complications—chapped nipples because she insisted on breast-feeding the baby, and other minor ailments—in fact kept her longer than that in Vienna. Alone at Maiernigg, Mahler found he could not work. Was it purely fortuitous, or did he need Alma's presence to be able to compose?

'The days pass, and I get nothing down on paper', he wrote to Alma, in between two strict injunctions as to how she was to look after herself. He was experiencing one of his composer's blocks, and it worried him. Alma arrived at last, with her mother and the two children. The new baby Anna was enchanting. She gazed at the world through eyes so wide, so blue, that they nicknamed her Gucki (*gucken*: to peep). And Mahler immediately began to compose again, feverishly. The crisis was over.

The summer passed peacefully. Alma found it hard to understand how Mahler could compose more *Kindertotenlieder* when his two little daughters were there, warm and tender. But Anna Moll's presence was reassuring, and they had visitors: Bruno Walter and Erika Conrat, the daughter of a Viennese industrialist, who has left an idyllic account of the few days she spent at Maiernigg.

In her honour Mahler was less uncouth than usual, and agreed to go with them by boat to take tea. 'The arrival there and the tea were a veritable torture for me', she wrote. 'That beautiful young woman, that famous man whom everyone knows! On the way back, I was sitting opposite Alma. Her hair gleamed bright in the setting sun. She looked like a superb wild animal. What a fine couple they make!'

Alma wrote little during this period, which was always a good sign.

But later she described those days at Maiernigg, when for some reason or other Mahler chose to work on the top floor of the house instead of in the Häuschen. Then there had to be absolute silence on all floors. The children were shut in their room, the cook warned not to stir hand or foot. 'I no longer played the piano, I no longer sang, I no longer moved . . . I had completely renounced my own existence, my own wishes, even though it grieved me enormously to do so.'

And, recalling those summer days, she added: 'For him, I had remained a young girl, in spite of the children and constant pregnancies. But he saw me first and foremost as his comrade, the mother of his children, his housewife, and was to discover what he had lost too late. These carnivorous geniuses who firmly believe they are vegetarians!' Did she love this carnivorous genius? Perhaps, but, oh, how she hated him!

That summer, in 1904, Mahler completed the Sixth Symphony and took Alma out to the Häuschen to play it to her. And for the first time she was moved by his music. Her eyes filled with tears.

But in September, back in Vienna, she learnt that Klimt was getting married, and it came as a shock to her.

Klimt getting married! My youth is over. Mother told me yesterday. I kept quite calm. I don't begrudge them their happiness, that is to say I am a bit jealous. He was so close to me . . . I am so grateful to him for having awakened me. As for her [the lady in question was the dressmaker Emilie Flöge], she is without fault, immaculate. Her beauty, her charm, all that is perfect. Apart from that, she is a nobody.

Whereas with me nothing has faded, neither my looks, nor my mind, nor my talent. I am neither happy nor unhappy. I have suddenly realized that I am leading only a semblance of a life.

Inwardly I feel completely frustrated. My ship is in port, but it's leaking.

She was 25 years old.

Clearly, the Mahler couple were going through a difficult period. He had lost patience with his wife's moodiness. 'Is it because your beautiful, elaborate dreams have not come true?' he asked, sarcastically. Sometimes she blamed herself and sometimes him.

'Yesterday we were discussing the past and by chance I mentioned that I found his smell unpleasant when we first knew each other. He replied: "That's the key to a lot of things. You acted against your nature." I alone knew how right he was . . .'. What a pleasant conversation between husband and wife! They both suffered under the financial economies Alma had imposed on them. He would sing, paraphrasing one of Weber's heroes: 'I put my trust in God and in thee to get us out of debt!' But in the mean time she was refusing invitations because she had nothing to wear, and he was tired of having to count the cost of everything he bought.

When did she begin to drink? It is impossible to say precisely. Her friends only noticed that when she was invited to dinner she drank enough to become overexcited. Some years later this tendency became more pronounced. No one ever saw her really drunk, at the most tipsy. It seems that she began early to turn to the bottle for relief when depressed.

During the winter of 1905 Mahler clearly made an effort to bring a little animation into his wife's life, although his work at the Opera, combined with his travel commitments, was exhausting. Then sometimes he would sing *sotto voce* a refrain adapted from a popular opera: 'Oh happy, oh happy a tinker to be!'

The Mahlers now often lunched or dined in town, their hostesses boasting: 'He never goes anywhere, you know!' But he would get bored, and then, wrote Alma, 'he would emanate gloom and despondency as if there were a corpse under the table'. His presence was so intense that it spoke volumes even when he said nothing. Sometimes it was she who, under the influence of wine, let her tongue run away with her.

They entertained more often themselves. Hauptmann was a frequent guest, although Mahler didn't think much of his wife Grete. 'I feel sorry for poor Hauptmann,' he said, 'he's far too good for her. If she were my wife, she would have to sing small.' Dear Mahler, he was the one who would have to sing small, when the time came.

Meanwhile, there was a new arrival on the scene: Pfitzner, the young composer whom Alma had felt sorry for at the Krefeld Festival. Under the combined influence of Alma and Bruno Walter, Mahler had finally agreed to put on Pfitzner's opera, *Die Rose*. Pfitzner arrived in Vienna, puffed up with his own importance, to rehearse it. He was an officious, excitable, pretentious character. He considered Mahler's music to be 'thoroughly unpleasant', his wife highly attractive.

During the rehearsals of *Die Rose*, he became venturesome. One evening, finding himself alone with Alma, he got thoroughly excited, caressed her shoulders, kissed her hands, stroked her bosom. She pushed him off, not too roughly, and noted: 'He was very amorous . . . I liked it. My skin tingled under his touch in a way it had not done for so long.' Ah well! Alma was a woman!

Mahler, jealous, was 'morose and uncommunicative'. 'He said I always sided with the others. And he was right. At heart we are now strangers to each other. He came to sleep with me. Neither of us knew exactly why. He said: "Just read the *Kreutzer Sonata!*" The story, remember, is of a husband deceived who stabs his wife.' Jealousy caused Mahler to do strange things. He kept on inviting Pfitzner to his house, and would then go out, leaving him alone with Alma. Did he want to offer her a lover? Or provoke a showdown?

A comic scene occurred on 1 May. While Mahler was working, at the Opera, on *Die Rose*, Pfitzner left the rehearsal saying he had an urgent appointment. He called at a florist's, bought a red rose, and took it to Alma. But on the way, on the Ring, he bumped into a workers' procession, and, confronted with the horrendous sight of the proletariat on the march, he took to his heels, arrived breathless at the Auenbruggergasse, and took refuge in Alma's room, persuaded that the red cohorts were after him.

Then Mahler arrived, and saw at once the nature of Pfitzner's urgent appointment. But he was in such a good humour that, suddenly, he couldn't have cared less. He too had come across the workers' procession. He had marched along with them for a moment, and had exchanged fraternal greetings with them. Truly, they were his brothers! 'Those men', he said, 'are the future.'

'And there they were,' Alma concluded in her diary, 'two men arguing for hours, neither prepared to give an inch to the other, and I was in between.' There is no doubt that, that day, Alma's instincts made her side with Pfitzner. Beautiful Alma was not exactly interested in social questions, whereas Mahler's heart had always been on the left.

In May the Mahlers went together to the Strasbourg Festival (the city was then part of Germany), where they met Richard Strauss again. Mahler was due to conduct his Fifth Symphony and Strauss his 'Symphonia Domestica'. Strauss was his usual ebullient self.

After listening to a *cantatrice* singing Brahms, he burst out: 'That cow is just about good enough to sing in a cabaret. Asking for an encore! Tiring my woodwinds already at their last gasp! But that's what you'd expect with a big shot like Brahms! If I finished my symphony with a perfect C major chord, I'd bring the house down too!' The singer's husband made a fuss and demanded redress. The affair concluded with a retraction in writing signed by Strauss and witnessed by the Mahlers.

They had some much pleasanter times with a group of French music-lovers who had made a special trip from Paris: the Clemenceaus, the mathematician Paul Painlevé (a future prime minister), and two army officers, Generals Picquart and De Lallemand. Picquart was a remarkable man from all points of view. He was the officer who had discovered the documents proving Captain Dreyfus's innocence and who refused to allow them to be swept under the carpet. Arrested, imprisoned, tried, condemned, and cashiered, he had been reinstated after Dreyfus's innocence had been proved.

He was also as it happened a music enthusiast, and played Mahler's symphonies as duets with his friend General De Lallemand. While in prison he had promised himself that if he survived he would go on a pilgrimage to all the places Beethoven had stayed at (Beethoven being the man he admired the most in the world) and that he would hear *Tristan and Isolde* conducted by Mahler.

The second wish was to prove unexpectedly difficult to fulfil. On the afternoon in 1906 when Picquart was in Vienna with the Zuckerkandls, happily looking forward to the evening's entertainment, a telegram signed by Georges Clemenceau arrived for Berta: 'Please inform Picquart that I have just appointed him Minister for War. He must return at once.' Furious, Picquart managed all the same to hear the first act of *Tristan* before taking the train at the West Station.

He was a charming man, and spoke perfect German. The little group went on excursions looking for places where Goethe had been and discussed literature and music. A moment of grace, it would seem, in the sombre life of the Mahlers. And Richard Strauss sprang a surprise on them. He took them along to Wolff's, the Strasbourg music seller, and there, in the shop cluttered with pianos, and watched by curious bystanders peering in through the windows, he sang and played *Salome* to them. It was his third opera and he dreamt of seeing it performed in Vienna. The Mahlers were amazed. How strange that such music should come from Strauss . . .

That evening Mahler conducted Beethoven's Ninth with his own modifications to the orchestration. 'The finest performance I have ever heard in my life!' wrote Alma, always ready to enthuse when her husband was not conducting his own music. The audience went into raptures over his interpretation, though some thought it scandalous. Crowds of concert-goers rushed backstage to congratulate Mahler. He fled, Picquart and Clemenceau caught up with him and pushed him into a cab, and the evening ended merrily in a little tavern in the town.

Successes, distractions, stimulating conversations, the Strasbourg Festival was a ray of sunshine in the fog which shrouded Alma's heart and mind. The following month she was back at Maiernigg once more. While she was alone with the children, before he joined her, she was calm.

I worked all day, copying for Gustav. Being away from him opens my eyes. I really live, I live only in him. I copy for him, I play the piano to impress him. I learn, I read, all for the same reason.

And yet, when he is here, I poison most of my pleasures with my crises of hypersensitivity. That really deserves to be punished!

Again and again my feelings rebel, pride, ambition, the thirst for fame . . . instead of making his life sweet and beautiful, my one purpose here on earth.

Clearly, Alma had no illusions about herself. Her only illusion was about the ability of a human being to become someone different without suffering irreparable damage. And she made every effort to do just that.

No doubt she wrote to him about her struggle, for in one of his replies to her he wrote: 'I see that you are now on the right path'. But he had only to be there with her, and things went wrong. In her diary she confessed, devastatingly: 'Often, with Gustav, I can't find anything to say. I know exactly what he is going to reply before he opens his mouth.' Fortunately they had a lot of visitors that summer.

The following autumn Mahler was kept busy with preparations for a Mozart cycle, and also for a gala evening, a 'command performance' offered by the emperor to the king of Spain, Alphonse XIII. The programme consisted of the first act of *Lohengrin*, some scenes from *Lakmé*, and the first act of a ballet, *Excelsior*. That evening, in the director's box, Alma observed with astonishment the behaviour of the people of the Court, a world with which she was unacquainted.

First, when the audience were all in their seats, Mahler had to wait at the rostrum for a glance from the Prince Montenuovo, who himself had to wait for a signal from the Grand Master of Ceremonies, Wilhelm Nepallek, who was Alma's uncle. It was he who signalled, with a wave of his white cane, the arrival of the emperor and the King. 'I had the impression of having a lackey for a husband', Alma told Mahler after the performance.

Then, throughout the performance, the emperor kept up a steady undertone of conversation with his guests, who also chatted among themselves. This gala audience of courtiers displayed their indifference, if not scorn, for the artists on the stage or in the orchestra. Alma could not stand it. She left the theatre outraged.

Mahler, however, made the minimum of concessions to the Court. Alma told for example how he reacted when Prince Montenuovo recommended that he should re-engage the soprano Ellen Forster Brandt, whose voice was no longer good, but who had had a brief liaison with the emperor. 'So be it,' said Mahler, 'but I shall not put her name on the notices.' The prince insisted, explaining that the sovereign had promised the singer the engagement, which he would in any case pay for out of his personal coffers.

'Very well', said Mahler. 'But each time her name appears in the notices, it will be followed by the words: "By superior order of His Majesty"'. He had won. Innumerable anecdotes of this kind circulated in Vienna. 'Every time I go to see him', said Mahler, talking of Prince Montenuovo, 'he knows how far he can go, since at the slightest difficulty I offer him my resignation.'

But in the autumn of 1906 he was tired. He was hated by most of the musicians in the orchestra because of his peremptory treatment of them, and subjected to a barrage of criticism which steadily increased in intensity. They reproached him for not performing more new works, they reminded him that he had been appointed to direct the Opera, not 'to promote his own works here and in other countries', they criticized his 'sergeant-major tone of command'. One leading music critic wrote: 'He has all the abilities necessary to direct the Opera because of his undeniable genius, but has become the victim of his own inflated ego and neurotic disposition. The administration of our Opera should be entrusted to someone who is sound in mind, not to an arrogant artist whose health is poor.'

It was an old story, the director had fallen out of fashion, as he himself put it. At least that was how he saw it. He summed up the situation in these words to a journalist, after he had given up his job: 'The Court was on one side, the press on the other, the public was here, my family was there, and finally, there was also the enemy in my own breast. Often it was very painful.'

At a concert in Linz, his First Symphony was so badly received, so stupidly criticized that he cancelled the second concert, and wrote to Alma: 'Why should I always let myself be pissed on. Am I a lamp-post?'

He travelled to Berlin, and found that the press there was full of rumours of his coming resignation. Since he had been appointed by the Emperor, he could only lose his post if he resigned. But the rumours worried him. 'So there are other people too who would like to see the back of me as soon as possible . . . How lucky that we are at least able to count on our 50,000 florins of savings, and the annual pension of 5,000.' This remark confirms that Alma's plan had been carried out. The Mahlers were free of debt.

Back in Vienna, he found the press in full cry announcing his departure. But Prince Montenuovo was assuring his visitors that nothing of the sort had even been considered. Mahler found himself in a very strong position again after staging the *Valkyrie*, with settings by the stage-designer Alfred Roller, a 'Secessionist' with whom he had already worked.

Of his production of the *Valkyrie* the conductor Otto Klemperer said later: 'It is difficult to talk of that performance other than to say that it achieved absolute perfection, that one could not find words to describe it.' But Mahler was at the end of his tether. Throughout this stormy period Alma had effectively carried out her role of 'companion', of affectionate associate when the going was rough. In May, Schönberg, scandalized by the treatment the press was inflicting on Mahler, wrote to Karl Kraus asking him to defend Mahler. Kraus did nothing.

Finally, in May 1907, Mahler resigned, and Alma ran to the

telephone to break the news to Berta Zuckerkandl. To Berta she sounded, if not happy, at least relieved. Now she would use all her influence to ensure that, of the many offers that arrived as soon as Mahler's decision was known, it would be the post at the New York Metropolitan Opera House that he would consider first.

These events did not pass without repercussions. Vienna took up the cudgels for or against Mahler's departure. A group of intellectuals and artists sent an 'open letter' to Mahler supported by seventy-two signatures, including those of Klimt, Schnitzler, Hofmannsthal, Stefan Zweig, and Max Burckhard. Prince Montenuovo tried to make Mahler change his mind because he could not find an adequate replacement for him. The main Viennese daily, the *Neue Freie Presse*, conducted a campaign also advocating this course. But things had gone beyond the point of no return. Mahler had finished with Vienna.

'I'm leaving because I can no longer stand this rabble', said Mahler in a letter to an old friend, the physicist Berliner. It must also be said that, in New York, where he had contracted to spend three months a year for four years, his financial rewards would be much higher than his annual salary at the *Hofoper*. It was agreed that he would go to the United States in November. Meanwhile, after those agitated spring months, the Mahlers went off to spend the summer in Maiernigg.

And there, at the end of June, the drama occurred. The elder of the two daughters, Putzi, now four and a half years old, fell ill with diphtheria. The vaccine against diphtheria had not yet been developed and it was a fatal disease. Putzi struggled for fourteen dreadful days and nights. One evening, she was unable to breathe, and the doctor decided to do a tracheotomy to give her relief. He operated then and there. She lived another twenty-four hours, and then it was all over.

Alma picked up the dead child in her arms, carried her to her own bed, and collapsed, prostrate, by the bedside. Mahler, sobbing violently, ran hither and thither. They rushed to the telephone to call Anna Moll, who came at once and found them utterly distraught. That night the three of them slept in the same room, because they could not bear to separate.

For Mahler, the child's death was pure tragedy. Of the two daughters, she was the one who resembled him, with her black curls and determined character. 'They used to have long conversations. No one knew what they talked about. I never disturbed them', wrote Alma.

We had a fussy English governess who would take the child spruce and tidy to the door [of the Häuschen]. Some time later, Mahler would reappear holding her by the hand. She was then usually sticky with jam from head to foot and I had to calm the Englishwoman. But they returned such a united couple and so happy with their conversation that I too was pleased to see it, though I said nothing. She was completely his child, radiantly beautiful, stubborn, and at the same time unapproachable, so much so that it might have become a problem. Her black curls and her great blue eyes . . . She was not granted long to live but that was how it had to be. She was destined to be his joy for a few years, and that in itself was worth an eternity.

Two days after Putzi's death, as the little coffin was being carried away, Anna Moll was taken ill and Alma fainted. The doctor examined her, and ordered her to rest and stay in bed. 'While you're at it, doctor,' said Mahler, 'would you mind examining me too? My wife is constantly worrying about my heart . . . '. Doctor Blumenthal nodded, knelt beside the sofa on which Mahler had lain down, got up, looked grave, and said: 'Well, a heart like that is nothing to be proud of!'

He went no further with his diagnosis. The Mahlers and Anna talked it over. Suppose he was wrong? Or exaggerating? They decided to seek a second opinion at once, from Professor Kovacs who had looked after Alma. Then, whatever the verdict, they would give up Maiernigg. The very sight of the place had become unbearable, after those last harrowing days.

An appointment was made. Mahler went back to Vienna alone, was seen by Professor Kovacs, and sent a telegram to his wife. The doctor had diagnosed a 'bilateral but compensated contraction of the heart valves', on the basis of which he had ordered Mahler to give up at once all physical effort. This came as a violent shock for Mahler, who had always been a great walker, swimmer, and cyclist. From now on he would be afraid of every gesture, every step he took.

In fact, it is now believed that Mahler was suffering from acute articular rheumatism resulting from a streptococcal angina contracted in his childhood. But in those days cardiology was still in its infancy. What with Putzi's death, the grim spectre of his own death, and the ban on all physical effort imposed on him, it was a broken man who went to spend a few days in the Tyrol with his wife, Gucki, and the governess. Incidentally, little Gucki, who died in 1988 at the age of 84, was haunted all her life by her sister's death, which she believed was her fault. A not unusual phenomenon, but hard to live with nevertheless.

Mahler forbade Alma to wear mourning on the grounds that she must not do 'anything that played to the gallery'. He never spoke of Putzi to anyone. Bruno Walter, after meeting them, wrote to his parents: 'He is quite devastated. She seems to me to be bearing up better, aided by tears and philosophy.' Had the drama they had lived through brought them closer together? No. Obscurely, silently, Mahler felt his wife was to blame. But for the time being Alma forgot the more complex reasons she had for weeping.

Maiernigg was sold up, Mahler fulfilled a few more engagements involving some travelling, and then the time came at last to leave Vienna for New York. His last visit was to the Zuckerkandls, the only friends he would have liked to take with him. 'I am taking my homeland with me,' he told them,

my Alma and my child. Now that the heavy burden of work has at last been lifted from my shoulders, I know what my future task will be. Alma has sacrificed ten years of her youth for me. No one knows or can ever know with what devotion she has sacrificed her own life to me and to my work. It is with a light heart that I set off on my travels with her.

To their surprise a number of people were waiting on the platform of the West Station to see them off. The group included Schönberg, Webern, who had organized the send-off, Alban Berg, Klimt . . .

In Paris they were met by their French friends, the Clemenceaus, and a young Russian pianist, Ossip Gabrilovich, whom they had met in St Petersburg. According to Emil Zuckerkandl, Gabrilovich, with his distorted features, looked like 'a Kiev Jew after a pogrom'. But he was also a fanatical admirer of Mahler, and succumbed at once to Alma's fatal charm.

Some days passed, and then, one evening, in the drawing-room of the suite the Mahlers occupied at the Hotel Bellevue, he could stand it no longer and declared his passion in an original way. 'I must confess something terrible to you. I am in the process of falling madly in love with you. Help me to escape from myself! I like Mahler and would hate to upset him.' How did Alma react?

So, after all, I was still worthy of being loved, I was neither old nor ugly as I had thought. In the semi-darkness he groped to find my hand. But the light went on. Mahler was there, in the room, full of goodness and love, and the spell was broken. Nevertheless, for some time to come that scene helped me to overcome many an attack of inferiority.

A man who desires you, what better tonic than that? She needed it, after five years of marriage.

Ossip was to turn up again, a little while later. But it was not he but another man who would set in train Mahler's martyrdom, Alma's resurrection, and the astonishing reversal in their psychological relationship to each other.

For the time being Alma still admired her difficult husband, even though he irritated her. And he had full confidence in her ability to handle the material problems of their life together. More than that, in this young woman of 25 he had found a mother.

In those last weeks Alma had no time for the sessions of introspection, self-depreciation, and questioning as to the meaning of her life which usually filled her diary. When she embarked, at Cherbourg, she was happy to leave Vienna behind her, and excited at the prospect of getting to know New York. She accompanied her genius of a husband across the ocean in an optimistic frame of mind. He suffered from seasickness, she enjoyed the voyage.

6. Social Life and Servitude

Whether in 1907 or today, arriving in New York by boat is always an exhilarating experience. But very soon after the Mahlers came down the gangway from the SS *Augusta Victoria*, Gustav was fully absorbed in rehearsals at the Metropolitan. He had chosen to begin with a production of *Tristan and Isolde*.

And again Alma was alone. Completely alone. Going for walks in Manhattan was pleasant enough, but she had soon had enough of that. Moreover, she could not speak a word of English. Her talents did not extend to foreign languages. And she had left Gucki behind to be looked after by her grandmother. What could she find to do, all day long?

They were staying in a good hotel—the Majestic—but kept entirely to themselves. Mahler, who now avoided the slightest physical effort, stayed in bed as long as possible in the morning. They took all their meals in their room. The hotel reception was instructed never to put calls through to their suite, since Mahler could not bear to be disturbed. He had greatly changed. But he was more 'liveable with', even though he still strummed nervously on the table, pawed with his feet like a wild boar, and startled people with the suddenness of his remarks.

As is so often the case, the death of his favourite child had altered the relative importance of a lot of things for him, including preparations for a performance of *Tristan and Isolde*. Alma, for her part, found this cloistered existence stifling, and soon fell ill. In fact her constitution was solid as a rock, and she was to reach the age of 85 before an attack of pneumonia carried her off. But as a young woman she suffered repeatedly from mysterious illnesses. She attributed them variously to nerves or to heart trouble. These indispositions baffled her doctors, and were, as is now widely accepted, the means whereby her body expressed the rebellion of her mind.

This time, however, her 'illness' proved to be more than psychological in origin. She had a miscarriage. Once it was over, she remained as depressed as ever. To make a change for her, Mahler accepted one or two invitations which enabled them to meet some Americans, such as the financier Otto Kahn, one of the patrons of the Met. At his home they got to know the President of the Neurological Society, Doctor Fraenkel, a picturesque character who became a close friend and later even proposed to Alma. Yet another one!

Evenings at the Met, going with Mahler to a guest performance given by him in Philadelphia, visits to people from Vienna living in New York—things were improving somewhat for Alma. And, above all, since Putzi had died Alma had an objective reason which even in her eyes took precedence over her other grounds for depression, and ennobled, as it were, her tears when she gave way to fits of weeping.

Both the Mahlers wrote lots of letters, especially to their friends in Vienna. They gave no indication of homesickness, quite the contrary indeed. 'Something quite new for me, after the harsh treatment I received in Vienna', wrote Mahler to his mother-in-law, 'is the way everyone is so full of good wishes and gratitude for the few things I have so far been able to do.

'I live like a prima donna. I feel that I am someone important, and hope that America, so widely reputed to be a dreadful place, will continue to treat me well.' When the Mahlers left to return to Europe at the end of their first New York season, and landed at Hamburg in April 1908, the thought that they would soon be going back for a second visit was by no means an unwelcome one. They liked America.

That summer Mahler composed what was perhaps his most important work, *The Song of the Earth*. It was in fact a symphony, his ninth, but he avoided calling it that for superstitious reasons: Beethoven, Schubert, and Bruckner had all died after composing their ninth symphonies.

After much searching Alma and her mother had found a house in Toblach (Dobbiaco) in South Tyrol. It was a substantial house whose owner rented out the first floor, ten rooms into which the family moved with two servants, a governess, and three pianos. Again a Häuschen had been built for Mahler to work in. The surrounding country was beautiful, the view magnificent.

Concerning the moving-in, Alma later wrote:

The way it was decided who or what was to go where was wondrous to behold. We led him proudly from room to room, and after much toing and froing, he chose for himself the two largest and nicest rooms. Then we looked all over the house to find the largest bed and had it moved there, although he was shorter than I. He was blissfully unconscious of his own selfishness, he would have been quite terrified if he had realized it. My mother and I followed him round, enjoying the spectacle of his innocent pleasure.

We then had the two grand pianos installed, and an upright in the hut in the garden, his workroom. And now at last we could settle down to a life of peace and quiet, occasionally interrupted by visits from friends.

Visitors in fact came thick and fast. One such was Ossip Gabrilovich, the young Russian pianist, who arrived with his brother. He was, of course, still in love with Alma. 'My feelings, temporarily at a loose end, got somewhat involved with those of that young man', wrote Alma. 'It had become obvious that we had rather fallen for each other. We didn't want to admit it, and fought hard against it.'

One evening, however, they kissed by moonlight. 'Just the one kiss, and Gabrilovich went away.' But not for ever. He was to turn up again in New York.

Burckhard was not very far away. He was at St Gilgen on the Wolfgangsee. But he was in no state to visit her. With a gesture of compassion rare for Alma, she went to him. When she arrived at the little house surrounded by water where he had cut himself off to avoid being seen by anyone, he said: 'My condition must be pretty bad for Mahler to let you come and see me.' The man who had formed—and deformed—Alma's mind, whose influence over her Mahler detested, and who had once said: 'If someone needs help, don't give it to him. He isn't worthy of it'—Burckhard, the disciple of Nietzsche, was to fight a lonely battle with death for many long months to come.

In spite of the frequent comings-and-goings at Toblach, Alma described that summer of 1908 as 'the saddest and most painful we

had ever or would ever spend together . . . full of sorrow for the child
we had lost, full of worries about Mahler's health'.

Before leaving again for the United States, Mahler still had
several engagements to fulfil. One was in Prague, where he was to
conduct the première of his Seventh Symphony. For that occasion
Alma went with him. She was as unreceptive as ever to her husband's
music, and this certainly did not pass unnoticed. A Swiss journalist,
William Ritter, observed her during the final rehearsal, and concluded
that the beautiful Frau Mahler, 'the idol of her husband', was
incapable of appreciating either the genius 'who agonized with love
before her' or the work she had just heard, which was, after all,
'completely dedicated to her'.

Mahler's following engagements took him to Munich, and then to
Hamburg. From the train, he wrote: 'I was so sorry to leave you
indisposed, indeed to leave you at all. This time it was only because
of your "three days", otherwise I wouldn't have done it for the
world.' It seems that these 'three days' each month played a role in
Alma's life that would nowadays be considered disproportionate.
But here again perhaps the mind was no stranger to the things the
body seemed to be saying.

Finally the time came for them to leave for New York. They
embarked this time at Cuxhaven, with Gucki, now 4 years old, and
her governess Miss Turner. On the tender which took them out to
the liner Gucki, wide-eyed with wonderment, began jumping up and
down. 'Don't get excited!' said the governess, 'don't get excited!'
Whereupon Mahler picked up his daughter, sat her down where she
could look over the side, and said: 'Now go on, get excited! You must
get excited!' New York was on the other side of the water.

That second season in America was, on the whole, a pleasant one.
This time the Mahlers stayed at the Savoy on Fifth Avenue, a hotel
frequented by several artists from the Metropolitan, including Caruso,
of whom Alma wrote that, 'even as a human being, he was a genius'.
They had a good suite on the eleventh floor. And what was more,
they did not shut themselves off in it.

Mahler, less tyrannical and despotic than in Vienna, had a more
serene approach to the problems he encountered in his work. The
Met now had two star-conductors, Mahler and Toscanini. The

ebullient Italian wanted to conduct the entire repertory. He had already 'stolen' *Tristan* from Mahler. The two men could not stand each other—which was only normal. But Mahler stayed relatively calm, and was less worried about his health. And he and Alma were launched into the whirl of New York fashionable society.

In the account she gives of that 1908–9 season, Alma waxes ecstatic over American hospitality, including that of the old Mayflower families who invited them as guests.

When he felt like it, Mahler accompanied me, and got more enjoyment out of those occasions than one would have imagined. He never missed a dinner. Besides, over there they manage these things differently from us . . . At ten we were already back at home, without being tired, having met new faces, new personalities who in their turn invited us to visit them. With the result that we were involved in a never-ending social round.

No doubt about it, things were looking up for Alma, and now she no longer had to worry about not having suitable clothes to wear. But deep down in herself . . .

And then who should turn up again but the ugly pianist, Ossip Gabrilovich! What took place between them? Nothing very serious, apparently. The young man was full of scruples, so they put on a great display of noble sentiments for each other.

One evening he came to see them, at the hotel. They dined together. Mahler then retired to his room, leaving Alma and the young pianist together in the salon. He played for her the little Intermezzo in A major by Brahms which she liked so much. Once again they launched into a long exchange of passionate assurances of longing for each other, coupled with admissions of the need for self-denial. No, it was impossible, they had no right, etc. In dominating their mutual desire they thought each other sublime. He played the little Intermezzo again one last time, as a final farewell. And took his leave.

Suddenly Mahler was standing in the doorway. Torturing himself, he tortured her. He had been listening the whole time. Now he wanted to know what there had been between Alma and Ossip. A long argument ensued, in which Alma finally managed to convince her husband that she had done nothing wrong. He calmed down at last, and returned to his room. Alma went to the window, opened it, and stood there listening to the street noises coming up to her on the eleventh floor, the idea of suicide playing in her mind: to jump, to come smashing down, to finish with life . . . She remained standing there at the window all night long.

'But, as always, a new day dawned. And as the milky mist of an early autumn morning in New York began to clear, I found myself again.' The following year Ossip Gabrilovich married the singer Clara Clemens, Mark Twain's daughter.

Anna came over from Austria. Mahler had repeatedly urged her to join them. She arrived just in time. All the signs indicate that in the midst of their many social engagements Alma had again had a miscarriage. Gustav wrote to Carl Moll: 'Alma is very well. I think she herself wrote to you about her condition. She has been freed of her burden. This time she too is disappointed.' Alma had not finished with the business of child-bearing, far from it. But her subsequent pregnancies were part of another life.

Mahler himself had had a bad attack of flu. But when they left New York amidst flowers and laudatory press notices, he had a new contract in his pocket. A group of wealthy music-loving ladies had decided to set up a permanent orchestra in New York, and to ask Mahler to direct it. Thus was founded the subsequently renowned New York Philharmonic Orchestra. Meanwhile, *en route* for Vienna, the Mahlers broke their journey in Paris, where the Molls had organized a little surprise for them. They had commissioned Rodin to make a bust of Mahler.

The two men knew nothing of each other. Mahler had simply been told that Rodin wished to sculpt a head of him, while the Clemenceaus had contacted Rodin and negotiated a reasonable price. Everything went off very well, but after nine or ten sittings Mahler grew impatient and went away, promising that he would return. They resumed their journey to Vienna.

It would be too simple, derisory even, to regard Alma as no more than a young woman condemned to a life of boredom whose morale could be restored by the bright lights of a New York season and a few amusements in Paris. Activities that took her out of herself were beneficial, but totally inadequate to resolve the profound contradiction she continued to feel between her aspirations for a life she could properly call her own and the state of feudal servitude in which Mahler kept her. To say nothing of her sexual deprivation.

Back in Vienna she wrote the following lines to her friend, the musicologist Guido Adler, to explain why he had not heard from her for so long: 'In the past twelve months I have had a terrible time, one painful upset after another.' Even when allowance is made for her propensity to exaggerate whenever she had a pen in her hand, that is not the kind of thing a happy, contented woman would write. Was she perhaps suffering from some of those disorders generally termed 'feminine' which typically cause mental depression? However that may be, she was sent off to take a cure at Levico, near Trento. She arrived there with Gucki and Miss Turner. Mahler meanwhile stayed at Toblach, and grew worried when he received only sad little letters from her indicating no improvement in her condition.

In one of his letters to her, after observing that the cure at Levico was not proving 'very effective in calming your nerves', he added these pathetic words: 'In spite of all my prayers and supplications I still do not know what is the matter with you!' One can imagine how many times he must have said: 'But look, what is wrong with you?' with all the possible tones and variations a husband-and-wife relationship can give rise to.

During her stay in Levico, which bored her to death, he wrote her long philosophizing, moralizing letters which could only have made her depression more complete. Had she complained that she could not compose any more? Apparently, since in one of his replies he writes: 'Of course I am not saying that creative work is superfluous. It is something people must have for their development, and for the happiness which is also a sign of health and the creative urge. But why does it have to be music?' In other words, if she wanted to paint, he would have no objections at all! The whole object of the letter was to explain to her the transitory nature of human works. The only thing that was lasting was 'what a person makes of himself through struggle and unceasing activity'. As Alma put it later: 'We wrote to each other, but only about abstract subjects.'

While he was alone at Toblach, he managed somehow to have domestic problems with the cook, and above all with the chambermaid Kathi, who went as far as to write to Alma to complain. Alma reacted vigorously and so did Mahler. As Alma remarked, no one can match the defenders of the human race when it comes to bungling their relationships with their subordinates.

She returned at last, still suffering. Richard Strauss and his wife were passing through Toblach, and invited the Mahlers for dinner at their hotel. Pauline greeted them loudly in the hotel entrance with: 'Hallo, Mahler. How goes it? How was America? Lousy, what? I hope you managed to squeeze them for a dollar or two.' There was nobody like Pauline. At table Strauss asked Mahler to sit next to Pauline. She protested: 'Only so long as you don't start that dreadful fidgeting! I can't stand it!' A dreadful fellow, Strauss! But that same dreadful Strauss was working that summer on a new opera, *Der Rosenkavalier*, libretto by Hofmannsthal. Creative genius is a mysterious thing.

In October, *en route* once again for the United States, the Mahlers stopped off in Paris so that Rodin could complete his bust of Gustav. They stayed in style this time at the Hotel Majestic. Mahler sat three or four times. In November Carl Moll came to Paris to decide with Rodin which of the plaster casts should be used for the final bronze.

And then they were plunged once again into the social whirl of New York. One evening the Mahlers were invited to dinner by the bank magnate, Otto Kahn. Doctor Fraenkel was there. Their host took them to see the medium, Eusapia Palladino. The celebrated Italian lady caused the strangest things to occur. Mysterious phosphorescent shapes floated through the air. A mandolin began to play, plucked by an invisible hand. The table lifted and moved. Objects fell over . . . And La Palladino whispered to Mahler that his life was in danger. He was visibly shaken, and went home that night profoundly disturbed.

Whatever one thinks of such experiments, in the interests of historical veracity it must be related that some years previously Pierre and Marie Curie also allowed their curiosity to get the better of them and went with Jean Perrin to see La Palladino. On that occasion, too, ectoplasm hovered in the air, objects moved of themselves, but the trickery involved was quickly discovered. Nevertheless Pierre Curie, far from sceptical in principle, continued to take a lively interest in spiritualism. And Eusapia Palladino went on to enjoy a brilliant international career.

Everything seems to have gone well for the Mahlers during that season in New York. Gustav wrote to Carl Moll: 'I'm looking fine, my weight is normal, and I can stand the enormous workload without

difficulty. Alma too is *much* better this year. The last few days she has
had fits of weakness again, but nowhere near as bad as last year.'

They went on a trip to Chinatown, venturing even into the
gambling and opium dens. 'In the stinking alleys,' writes Alma,
'those rats with long pigtails scuttled and darted along beneath the
walls. Mahler said: "I find it hard to believe that these are my
brothers"'. They also explored the Jewish quarter.

The difference in race was colossal. The Jews here work day and night shifts
so as not to waste an hour. The whole scene was hideous with old clothes
and rags. The smell of food hung in the air. I asked Mahler quietly, in his
own words: 'What about them? Are they our brothers?' he shook his head,
bewildered. Finally we turned the corner and could breathe more freely
again in a well-lit street for people like us. Is it really true that the only
differences are between classes, and not between races?

The Mahlers were also the guests of millionaires. One evening
they were invited by Louis Tiffany, the son of the founder of the
famous jewellery firm. All New York seemed to be there. The lavish
interior decorations left them speechless. Someone played the
Parsifal prelude on an organ. The host, a hashish addict, spoke a few
slurred, unintelligible words. The whole place seemed bewitched.

Servants glided noiselessly by bearing trays on which beautiful
glasses full of champagne made not the slightest tinkle', wrote Alma,
evidently fascinated by this feat. 'Palm trees, sofas, beautiful women
wearing strange shimmering dresses. It was like a dream, the
Thousand and One Nights in New York.' History does not record
whether the Mahlers asked themselves that evening: 'And are these
too our brothers?'

Anecdotes abound about the social life of the Mahlers in the
United States. They all show Gustav as an eccentric character who
would get up abruptly and go home in the middle of a meal, say the
most surprising things, or stubbornly refuse to open his mouth. But
everyone wanted to have him at their table. Did he get any pleasure
out of such social occasions? Or did he merely accept them because
he and Alma could no longer bear to be alone with each other, the
hardest of tests? Perhaps it was a combination of the two.

The pianist Samuel Chotzinoff has left his own impression of the
Mahlers in New York during that season. After the concerts he

would slip unobtrusively backstage 'to gaze with admiration at Mahler', but never daring to approach him. 'His wife was often with him. For me she was the most beautiful woman I had ever seen. In a way it seemed only right that Mahler, who was not good-looking and wore glasses, should have attracted such a beautiful woman by the force of his genius.'

Back in Europe, the Mahlers went first to Paris, where Gustav was due to conduct at a concert. Gabriel Pierné gave a dinner in his honour, and Alma found herself sitting between Debussy, who ate nothing, and Paul Dukas, who told her the famous story of the attempted suicide of the first Madame Debussy. Half-conscious, the poor woman had seen her husband come in, go through her pockets, and take her money before calling for a doctor. Understandably enough, as soon as she had sufficiently recovered she demanded a divorce.

Alma said later that Mahler had felt ill at ease and out of sorts the whole evening. Neither of them spoke much French, which cannot have helped.

On the following Sunday the auditorium of the Châtelet Theatre was filled to capacity. The audience included such distinguished personages as Countess Greffulhe, the Countess of Béarn, the Princess of Arenberg, the Clemenceaus and of course the two generals, Debussy and his wife, Paul Dukas, André Messager, and others.

Mahler was conducting his Second Symphony. According to Alma, whose account has been disputed, 'suddenly, in the middle of the second movement I saw Debussy, Dukas, and Pierné get up and leave the hall. The meaning of this gesture was obvious!' Obvious indeed, and not surprising as far as Debussy was concerned. He did not stand upon ceremony and was violently opposed to anything German. And Mahler's music was super-German. The audience at large applauded enthusiastically, however. But Mahler remained deeply offended by the attitude of his French fellow-musicians.

In Vienna the Mahlers went to stay with the Molls, now living in a new house, but still on the Hohe Warte. There they were saddened by a succession of bad news. In May their dear friend Emil Zuckerkandl died of cancer. Siegfried Lipiner, whom Mahler had been seeing again, also had cancer. And Max Burckhard was now in a desperate condition.

While Mahler, with Carl Moll, was busy searching the countryside around Vienna for a house to buy, Alma again began to complain of 'nervous troubles', and the doctors, clearly at their wits' end as to what was really wrong with her, sent her off to Tobelbad, a spa very much in fashion at that time. The last thing they could have guessed was that Alma would indeed find a remedy at the spa. But not in the thermal waters.

All married couples, including the happiest, have their problems, and periods when they hate each other. Alma and Gustav Mahler were held together by many things, first and foremost by music, which was the natural element for both of them, their oxygen. Mahler had confidence in Alma's musical instinct, she admired him as a conductor, he needed to have her by him when he composed, their intellectual interests overlapped and intertwined even though their philosophical and literary interests continued to diverge and she preferred Goethe to Dostoevsky. Mahler had grown less despotic, Alma more tolerant, more patient. Of any other married couple one would have said that after seven years of marriage their relationship was one of mutual affection.

But the self-denial that Mahler had exacted from Alma, and for which on occasion he expressed his gratitude to her, his insistence that he let herself be completely absorbed in him, and the way he had of treating her as an abstraction rather than as a woman of flesh and blood, all that had become literally unbearable for her. She was going to stop trying to bear it. And the explosion would be shattering.

7. Ruthless Queen and Obedient Subject

It all began at Tobelbad where Alma went to take the waters. Her daughter and Miss Turner accompanied her, and her mother was to join them later. Gustav wrote her a real loving husband's letter: 'You really are a stupid goose. Why do you torture yourself with such fantasies? I have never—really never—loved you so much as now. Get well quickly, my Lux, so that we can at last enjoy this world together like two good comrades, etc.'

He was working. He travelled to Leipzig, to Munich. What could she have written to him to elicit in reply a long dissertation on Plato? In his usual schoolmaster's style he wrote: 'Now at last you've grasped the essential point about Plato. In the Socrates speeches Plato is expressing his own view of the world which, misunderstood as "Platonic love", has filtered down over the centuries into the minds of even the least intelligent . . . '. A long development follows, and then this: 'This similarity between him and Christ comes readily to mind, and willy-nilly thinkers of all epochs have noticed it. . . . In both cases Eros is the creator of the world.'

In fact, as Mahler wrote those lines, Eros was having fun at his expense. He had materialized in the guise of a handsome, fair-haired, clear-eyed young man, the 27 year old son of an eminently respectable Prussian bourgeois family. His name was Walter Gropius, and he was on holiday at Tobelbad.

Later he became famous as founder of the Bauhaus, the celebrated school of architecture and applied art which gave us so much that is familiar in our present-day world, such as pre-fabricated building units, chairs made of steel tubes, walls of glass, and so on. In that summer of 1910 he stood at the beginning of his career as an architect, but he already had clear ideas of what he wanted to achieve. He gave lectures on improving productivity in factories by providing a better environment for the workers. The following year he would build for the Fagus-Werke at Alfeld a shoe-last factory in concrete, iron, glass, and yellow brick, a revolutionary building.

As usual, Alma's instinct did not fail her. Gropius was not just any young man. Unerringly she picked him out from the many who surrounded her. Was he taking a cure too? It was the fashionable thing to do at that time, and he was just recovering from a severe attack of flu. In any case, there he was at Tobelbad, and the doctor of the establishment introduced him to Alma. The affair progressed very rapidly, it would seem, under the protective wing of Anna Moll, who must have had her own ideas about what her daughter needed to cure her nerves.

From the first days of June to mid-July Alma and Gropius gave free rein to their passion. 'Once', wrote Alma later, 'we spent the whole night together, disturbed only by the light of the dawn and the sweet song of the nightingale. By my side lay a handsome young man. And that night two souls had found each other, their two bodies forgotten.' We have already noted that she was no poet! But despite the inflated style, she says what she means.

She suffered twinges of conscience, obviously. Who wouldn't? Of course she felt guilty. At night she made love with Gropius. During the day she wrote to her husband the 'sad little letters' that worried him. 'Are you hiding something from me? I always have the feeling that there is something between the lines.'

No doubt. Unconsciously she must have been dreaming of the moment when Mahler would know all. She let two days pass without writing. He grew worried, and then annoyed. 'I don't understand why you can't send me a postcard now and then. What on earth can one do with such a child-wife?' Alma a child-wife! He wrote to his mother-in-law telling her how worried he was about Alma and the 'torturing illnesses' she had to endure, adding: 'How lucky we are to have you!' He was the perfect cuckold.

In her diary, and in her autobiography, Alma suppressed all details of her first encounter with Walter Gropius. She refers only to a certain X who unfortunately fell in love with her during their walks together at Tobelbad. She left the spa, rejoined Mahler in Toblach, and 'about a week later a letter arrived from the young man in which he said he could not live without me, and that if I had the slightest regard for him I should give up everything and come to him'.

Not a word of that was true. After Alma left Tobelbad she corresponded regularly, via the poste restante, with her lover, until the day when the young man committed the most appalling blunder. He wrote Alma a passionate love-letter begging her to come away with him . . . and addressed it to Mahler, to Herr Direktor Mahler.

This act, for which Gropius himself was never able to provide the slightest explanation, was so extraordinary that there has been endless speculation as to its motivation. Gropius had always had a preference for affairs with married women whose husbands interested him. Was it Mahler he was in love with, through Alma? Or was he, in addressing the letter to him, unconsciously asking him to hand over Alma? The mystery of Gropius's 'absent-mindedness' has never been cleared up. But one thing is certain: it was no accident.

What happened then? The letter arrived and was put on the piano in the house. Mahler, returning from the Häuschen, saw it, opened it, read it, and called Alma. 'What does this mean?' he asked her, handing her the letter. She read it and suddenly let everything go. The things she had to say to him were terrible, though she did not raise her voice. Yes, she had deceived him, and with good reason. She, the lioness, held him there under her paw, the man who for the last seven years had lorded it over her, bullied her, frustrated her, stifled her, treated her like a disembodied spirit, crushed her beneath the weight of his blind genius. For a long time she had been overwhelmed with self-reproach, had often felt guilty for not being able to soar to the heights with him, had fought down her impulse to counter-attack, worse, had turned her aggressivity against herself. And now, suddenly, she could get it out of her system. 'At last, I could tell him everything!'

He showed neither anger nor bitterness, he made no accusations of infidelity. Inside him, the world was collapsing. Was she going to leave him as her lover was begging her to do? She said straight away that she would not. He felt guilty, guilty of having commandeered the life of a woman far too young for him. But when this crisis occurred he was 50, she 30. The root of the problem must now lie elsewhere. Where? What had happened? Their argument went on hour after hour, as arguments do in such crises. Mahler beat his breast, recalling all the renunciations he had imposed on Alma. He was so distraught that he appealed to his mother-in-law for help. And from that day onwards he never left Alma alone. He was jealous of everything and everybody. At night the door between their two rooms had to remain open, so that he could hear her breathing. Sometimes she would wake up and find him standing there, looking at her. One night she found him lying in the corridor where he had fainted.

Amid the ruins of his emotional life, one fear was uppermost: that he would lose Alma, that she would abandon him. The key to Mahler's attitude to his wife is probably to be found in the experience of his early years: a feeling of guilt and fear of being abandoned, the child's fear of losing his mother. But, after all, is the key so important? There he was, stricken and bleeding. He went to the hut and lay there sobbing on the floor . . .

And then Gropius turned up! Two days after the scene with the letter, Alma wrote to him, telling him that at all costs he must not come to Toblach. 'Because it [their affair] all came out by accident, as it were, and not by a spontaneous confession on my part, he has lost all confidence, all trust in me'.

But Gropius did not do as she asked. He arrived at the railway station, wandered around the village for a while, then walked out to their house. A guard dog chased him away. During a walk with Mahler, Alma caught sight of him, hiding under a bridge. And what did Alma do? She pointed him out to Mahler.

'I'll go and fetch him', said Mahler, and did just that. He went up to him and said, simply 'Let's go up to the house.' Night had fallen. The two men tramped up the dark country lane, one behind the other, neither speaking. When they arrived, Mahler called Alma and left her alone in the parlour with Gropius. After a while she grew worried and went to see if her husband was all right. She found him reading the Bible. He said: 'Whatever you decide will be right. Make up your mind.'

Should she leave her husband, go away with her lover, there and then, as he was urging her to do? Out of the question. Firmly, she told Gropius of her decision, and asked him to leave. Mahler, hat in one hand, lantern in the other, conducted Gropius to the edge of their property, again without a word. Later Gropius wrote to thank Mahler for the way he handled the encounter.

Had Alma enjoyed the way things had gone? It seems certain, for later she engineered other confrontations of this kind. The next day she went to Toblach to say goodbye to her lover. Did she make love with him in the hotel? Probably: she saw him to the train and he sent her telegrams from each station the train stopped at.

Alma's commentary: 'Long appeals followed, much imploring. Mahler used it all in the marvellous poems he wrote at that time . . . He was profoundly shaken. It was then that he wrote those exclamations and appeals to me on the manuscript of his sketches for the Tenth Symphony.'

On the manuscript of the Tenth Symphony Mahler wrote, 'O God, O God, why hast Thou forsaken me!' But also: 'You alone know what that means. Oh! Oh! Oh! Goodbye, my lyre!' and, finally, 'To live for you! To die for you, Almschi!' Twenty years later Alma's visitors in Vienna could admire those pages on display, in her drawing-room, like a hunting trophy.

Profoundly shaken by the Gropius episode, persuaded that he was going to lose Alma, Mahler now experienced the ultimate humiliation: he became impotent. Life became hell for him, confronted as he was with a young wife fresh from the arms of her lover. It was then that he made up his mind to consult Freud.

Freud was in Holland, on holiday with his family. One of Alma's cousins, the nerve specialist Richard Nepallek, got in touch with Freud to arrange an appointment. During the exchange of letters this involved, Mahler's condition worsened dramatically. When Alma awoke in the morning she would find on her bedside table notes, like this one:

Breath of my life! I have kissed your little slippers a thousand times, and stood with longing before your door. You have had mercy on me, goddess mine, but the demons have punished me again because I thought once more of myself and not of you, my darling.

I can't go away from your door and want to go on standing before it until I can hear the sweet sounds of you living and breathing.

Bless you, beloved, for all that you have given me . . . my every heartbeat is for you.

He was a long way from his weighty reflections on Plato.

Another day she found this note: 'My Almschilitzili, spend the day in bed today, that will be the best way for you to get some rest. I'll sit with you and stay at home all day.' One morning he left this message: 'Don't come out to me. It's too wet and your little feet could get damp—or put on galoshes.' The male domination on which their marriage relationship had been based was now turned upside down. Henceforth she was the ruthless Queen, he her obedient Subject.

He pushed the reversal even further, to the ultimate limit indeed. One day, returning from a walk with Gucki, Alma was stupefied to hear her Lieder being played and sung. She came into the room. Mahler, face lit up, was seated at the piano. He exclaimed: 'But what have I done! Your things are good! You must get to work again. We'll make a selection, and have them published at once. I shan't leave you alone until you have finished. My God, how pigheaded I've been!'

And off he went, playing them over again and again. It was high time he made the discovery. Some days later, he left her another note:

She loves me! My whole life is in those words. If ever I can't say that any more, I shall die. When I come up the stairs today, you won't be there. How I long to see you and take you in my arms, my darling, my sweetest beloved. My darling's songs, sweet harbingers of a divine being, shall be my stars until the sun of my life appears in my firmament!

It was certainly high time that Freud replied to Nepallek's letters. He finally agreed to see Mahler even though he was on holiday, but the patient would have to come to him. Mahler did not like the idea, put off the appointment twice, but finally took the train for Holland.

There are several accounts of the meeting between the two men. There is the description by Ernest Jones in his biography of Freud; Freud's own manuscript notes for his disciple, Marie Bonaparte; and Freud's written account to the psychoanalyst Theodor Reik, who was a passionate Mahler fan.

Mahler met Freud in a hotel, and then went on a four-hour walk with him through the streets of Leiden. Mahler knew nothing at all about psychoanalysis, which would imply an ignorance of contemporary thought which would be inconceivable today, when the Oedipus complex and its consequences are, or are thought to be, familiar ground for everyone. It was a complete eye-opener for Mahler therefore when Freud remarked: 'Your mother's name was Marie, I suppose? I've concluded that on the basis of various indications you gave during our conversation. How is it that you came to marry someone with another name?'

Mahler then remembered that he had always wanted to call Alma by her second name—which was Maria. He talked and talked for hours. Finally Freud reassured him. He knew Alma. The difference in their ages which so frightened Mahler was precisely what had made him so attractive to her. She had loved her father, and inevitably sought out that type of man. As for Mahler, he had looked for a woman who resembled his mother.

'Your mother was ill and care-worn', Freud told him, 'and that's how you would like your wife to be.' That was the account Mahler gave of his visit to Alma, and she, recording it in her diary, added: 'How right he [Freud] was in both cases. When he got to know me, he would have liked me to be more marked by suffering—those were his very words . . . And I really had always been looking for a short, stocky man with the wisdom and intellectual superiority I had known and loved in my father.'

Freud, who was not interested in music, passed on to Marie Bonaparte one piece of information which was bound to make the musicologists' blood boil.

In the course of the conversation Mahler suddenly said that he now understood why his music in its noblest passages, precisely those inspired by the deepest feelings, could never attain the perfection he aimed at, because some snatch of popular music got in between and spoilt everything. His father, a brutal man apparently, had treated his wife very badly, and when Mahler was still a little boy a particularly painful scene took place between them. The boy couldn't bear to see it, and ran out into the street. Just at that moment a barrel organ started up with the well-known Viennese tune 'O du lieber Augustin'. Mahler believed that from that time onwards high tragedy had been inextricably linked with superficial comedy in his mind, the one mood inevitably bringing the other with it.

Whether Mahler was right or not about his particular creative process, those four hours of instant psychoanalysis helped him. Freud wrote later to Theodor Reik:

I spent an afternoon in Leiden analysing Mahler, and if the reports are to be believed, I helped him a lot. He came to see me because his wife at that time had rebelled at the withdrawal of his libido. In the course of interesting incursions into his life history we discovered his love requirements, in particular his Marian complex (mother fixation). I had occasion to admire his marvellous readiness of understanding. No light was thrown on the symptomatic façade of his obsessional neurosis. It was as if we had sunk a single deep shaft through a mysterious building.

Four hours, even with Freud, did not constitute an analysis, of course. Nevertheless, it gave Mahler relief, and even permitted the return of the aforesaid libido. In other words he was again capable of making love to a wife who had 'rebelled' against his impotence.

Alma, on the other hand, was profoundly worried. In her letters to Gropius from Toblach she described the transformed Mahler who now overwhelmed her with the display of his love. 'I am experiencing something at my side that I would not have believed possible. Namely, that [his] love is so boundless that my staying here—in spite of all that has happened—means life, and my going away death to him . . . Gustav is like a sick, wonderful child.'

She wondered what to do, felt that she had to make up her mind, put questions to her lover: 'What arrangements would you make, what would happen to me if I decide on a life of love with you? Please help me, I don't know what I ought to do, or what my rights are.' Rights? Alma would not have been a woman of her time if she had committed adultery with a clear conscience. While she would never deny herself lovers, she would also always believe that illicit loves were guilty loves, which were sometimes punished as such. Yet the knowledge that the fruit was stolen made it taste the sweeter.

So she went on writing to Gropius from Toblach. She even asked him to introduce her to his mother. Anna Moll, 'understanding, patient, and discreet', served them as go-between, and thanks to her, it would seem, Alma even managed a trip to Vienna to see her lover.

In the last days of their summer in the mountains Mahler worked like a man possessed. But something had broken in him. This idolatry, this admiration he now has for me, are definitely not normal', wrote Alma to Gropius.

She was infatuated with her good-looking lover. She told him so, and justified her infidelity to Mahler.

I know from the way my organism reacts that for the heart and all the other organs nothing is worse than forced asceticism. By that I don't mean only

1. *Alma Maria Schindler*

2. *Emil Jakob Schindler, 1842–92*

3. *Anna Schindler-Moll (née Bergen) with her daughters Alma (left)*
and Grete (right)

5. *Alexander von Zemlinsky*

4. *Alma, aged 10*

6. Alma, aged 27, with her two daughters

7. Gustav Mahler, aged 48

8. Oskar Kokoschka, 1908

9. Alma Mahler, 1909

10. *Gustav Klimt*

11. *Walter Gropius, in the uniform of a cavalry officer, during the First World War*

12. *Alma with Franz Werfel, France, 1940*

sensual pleasures, the loss of which has almost made me prematurely a lonely, resigned old woman, but also the continuing repose of my body ... I am now lying in bed ... you are by my side, I can feel you so intensely that you must feel me too.

In another letter she described the longing she felt: 'When will the time come when you are lying naked against my body, when nothing can separate us except perhaps sleep? I know that I am living only for the time when I can be completely and utterly yours.' That letter she signed, 'Your wife'. Others she signed, 'Your betrothed'.

The question arises: why did she not leave Mahler? For she did not leave him. Her marriage to Gropius took place much later, and in the interim she was to have other memorable love affairs.

She couldn't even envisage leaving Mahler. Why not? One possible explanation is that she knew that for her to leave him would be tantamount to killing him. But there could be another explanation: now that the situation was reversed and the Master had become the Slave she was finding an intense enjoyment in the new relationship. Her craving for respect, her appetite for domination, would now be satisfied. Both explanations could be right.

The Mahlers returned to Vienna. Alma saw Gropius again, of course, again with the discreet help of her mother. Alma wrote to him: 'My Walter ... I want a child by you.' She always had this reflex, the most natural thing in the world for a woman in love. 'Write and tell me if you too want that as strongly as you did a month ago ... '. He replied in lyrical vein: 'O joy of my life ... I have gone down on my knees before thee, O thou truth, and raised my eyes in gratitude to thee'.

At the beginning of September Mahler went off to the Munich Festival to conduct his Eighth Symphony. During the forty-eight hours of his separation from Alma, he wrote to her: 'Believe me, I am sick with love. If you remain away from me for a whole week, I shall surely die. Almschili, if you had left me then, I would simply have gone out like a torch deprived of air.' 'Sick with love' was about right.

When Alma joined him at the Hotel Continental, she found roses in every room of their suite. Many friends were there. But Justi and Countess Wydenbruck, an old friend of Mahler, behaved in a way that Alma considered to be 'unfriendly'. Mahler saw to it that they left immediately. Alma commented proudly: 'Mahler was no longer so inattentive. On the contrary, he watched now with burning impatience to see that people treated me with due respect and friendliness.' There is something frightening about those words.

While Mahler was at his rehearsals, Alma went to her lover, who was staying in the Regina Palast Hotel. The rehearsals were frequent and lengthy. The concert was a triumph for Mahler. That evening, at least, Alma was in the audience. Gropius slipped in discreetly and was disturbed by Mahler's music.

In November the Mahlers were due to embark at Cherbourg for the United States. It would be their fourth crossing. Mahler came from Bremen, Alma from Paris. She had found some excuse or other, with her mother's help, to come via Paris. The point was that she had a rendezvous with Gropius on the Orient Express. He was coming from Berlin, and would join it in Munich. Alma would board it in Vienna.

When the train drew in to the Munich Station, she was waiting for her lover, her face half-hidden behind her hat-veil, twisting a tiny handkerchief inside her muff. What if he didn't come? What if Mahler suddenly appeared? She had advised Gropius to book his place under a false name, but jealous husbands can be fiendishly clever. Behind the door of her sleeper, number 13, she listened to the sounds of the carriages being shunted together, the shouts, people walking on the platform ... The compartment door slid back and he was there!

What could be more romantic than the Orient Express? More erotic than a wagon-lit? They were blissfully happy, and their happiness continued for four more days in Paris. 'Those days in Paris—wonderful—not a care in the world the whole time'. But the time came for her to leave, to tear herself away. 'When shall I see you again as some god has created you—for only a god could have made you. I want to take all your beauty into myself. Our two perfections together must create a demi-god ... ', she wrote to him from New York. Her *idée fixe* again. Earlier she had written, about Mahler: 'To have a child by him: his mind, my body!'

Alma and Walter Gropius planned to meet again in Paris in March. It had been agreed that she would come back from the United States before Mahler to take care of arrangements for the house they were having built on the Semmering, outside Vienna.

Anna Moll, understandably worried about her daughter, wrote to the impatient Walter Gropius: 'I am quite sure that the love you two have for each other will survive all difficulties. I have complete confidence in you and am convinced that you love my child so much that you will do everything to avoid making her even more unhappy.' Her confidence was well placed. Through thick and thin Walter Gropius was, in every respect, perfect.

In New York Mahler threw himself once more into an intense round of activity with the Met and the Philharmonic. On Christmas Eve he organized a little ceremony for his wife. She found her table piled with presents and bestrewn with pink roses. He had even bought her perfume in spite of his aversion to it. There were also two vouchers: one 'To the value of 40 dollars, for a pleasant stroll along Fifth Avenue for Herr Gustav Mahler with his Almschili enjoying his Amschi's idea of the open air'; the other 'For the purchase of a solitaire to the value of more than 1,000 dollars, Gustav Mahler, New York, Christmas 1910.' She thanked him for the presents. But he was so sad that she had to comfort him.

Some days later the singer Frances Alda came to see them. She wanted to include one of Alma's Lieder in a concert she was giving. Mahler was at once wildly enthusiastic, and tried to persuade Alda to sing five Lieder, but the programme had already been fixed. Mahler decided that he would rehearse the Lied himself with the singer, and went with Alma to see her in her hotel, the Waldorf Astoria.

There he had something to say about every note. Frances Alda patiently obeyed his instructions. Mahler kept turning to his wife: 'Is that how you want it? And how about that phrase? Is that alright?' But Alma, suddenly overcome with timidity, hardly dared to open her mouth, and finally said: 'Don't ask me about that sort of thing. You know better than I.'

In her account of this episode, Alma added, 'At that time we were very united.' That is to say, since she had won the upper hand, she was in the best of moods. She had completely given up alcohol, and had even started composing again, as Mahler was proud to announce to his mother-in-law. 'Marvellous Lieder', he assured her. They were expecting her, he wrote, and urged her to come and join them without further delay. She would find Alma in the best of health.

But one morning Mahler complained of a sore throat. Against

Doctor Fraenkel's advice he went out. The next day he had a temperature. It was angina. Nevertheless, he insisted on going to Carnegie Hall, to conduct a concert. For a few days, he seemed to be better. Then the high temperature returned. This time he had to stay in bed.

For some weeks previously he had had differences of opinion with the patrons of the Philharmonic—for though he had calmed down, he was still as stubborn as ever—and the press put the most fanciful interpretations on his illness, some even alleging that it was only a pretence. In fact, Mahler had only three more months to live.

But no one suspected this, except perhaps Doctor Fraenkel. Mahler was suffering from a form of endocarditis, a sub-acute inflammation of the internal lining of the heart due to a streptococcal infection. The diagnosis was made by the foremost specialist in the field.

That was the beginning of long weeks of torturing anxiety, when every fall in temperature meant renewed hope, only to be followed by a relapse, when specialist after specialist was consulted, when they refused to admit, but finally had to admit, that every apparent improvement in the sick man's condition was only an illusion. Often Mahler was quite convinced that he would get better. Often he gave way to despair, and then was terrified of dying.

When he was feeling better he would say jokingly to Alma: 'If I kick the bucket, you'll make a good match for somebody. You're young, you're pretty. So whom shall we marry you off to?' He would go through a list of possible husbands, and then conclude: 'No, I'd better stay with you after all.'

During those weeks of suffering Alma lived up to the high idea she had of herself. She didn't stop writing to Gropius, whom she kept informed day by day of the latest developments, but she was attentive, tender, watchful, and practically never left the hotel. On the rare occasions when Mahler got up from his bed it was to lie on a sofa.

At the end of March, Alma wrote to Gropius:

To my great surprise I have managed the impossible. I literally haven't undressed for ten days. I have been nurse, mother, housewife—and above all full of pity, anxiety, and care. For the moment my sensibilities are numbed, but I know that when I see you everything in me will spring to life and blossom again. Love me, with those feelings that have made me so wonderfully happy. I want you! But you, do you want me?

On Doctor Fraenkel's insistence she took a day off from the sickroom and went to the Mendelssohn Hall to hear the concert in which Frances Alda sang her Lied. When she returned Mahler plied her with questions, saying that he had 'never been so excited at any of my own premières'. When he heard that Alma's Lied had been encored, he murmured: 'Thank God!'

As soon as she realized how serious things were, Alma turned to her mother for help. And the kindly Anna came, although she had another daughter, much younger, who needed her care. She entrusted Maria to her neighbours, and arrived. 'We knew that she would spare no effort, no trouble to come to Mahler when he called her', wrote Alma. 'Mahler's relationship with my mother and vice versa was so close that in earlier years I always used to say that if Mahler had come to Mama and said: "Look, I've had to kill Alma", she would simply have replied: "I'm sure you've done the right thing, Gustav", and wouldn't have asked him why.'

Anna took over from Alma by day at Gustav's bedside, Alma continuing to do the nights. He could not bear professional nurses near him. Alma fed him with a spoon, and he loved it. 'When I get better, we'll keep on with that', he said, 'It's so pleasant.'

The days went by. He lay there, 'wracked by a strange and fateful fever', knowing deep down that he was going to die. To revive his hopes, Doctor Fraenkel suggested that they should contact some of the celebrated European bacteriologists, and undertook the necessary steps. Mahler regained confidence. Alma began to pack their forty trunks and cases. On the day of their departure Mahler refused to take the stretcher that had been brought in, and, leaning on Doctor Fraenkel's arm, walked to the lift. The lift attendant turned away to hide his tears. The manager cleared the foyer to spare Mahler the curious stares of his clients.

He got on board the boat at last and lay down at once in his cabin, burning with fever. When they disembarked at Cherbourg the captain arranged for him to be shielded again from the gaze of the curious, behind the stacks of luggage on the tender which took them to the quayside. He was deathly pale. Going ashore was a long and painful process. On board a young man had volunteered to help them, but when they landed he had disappeared, and Alma only found him again on the train, telling stories to Gucki. It was Stefan Zweig, the writer. Alma never liked his works. He left an account of his impressions that day: 'He lay there, pale as a dying man, motionless, and with eyes closed. For the first time I saw him, the man of fire, weak. But his silhouette—unforgettable, unforgettable!—set against an unending greyness of sky and sea. Infinite sadness was in that sight, but also something transfigured by greatness, something moving slowly towards a perfect ending, like music.'

Finally the Mahlers, Anna, Miss Turner, and Gucki arrived in Paris, where Carl Moll was waiting for them. He had booked rooms for them in the Elysée Palace Hotel. The specialists whom Fraenkel had contacted from New York were away from Paris; it was Easter. A bacteriologist from the Pasteur Institute, Professor André Chante-messe, agreed to return from the Auvergne, where he was on holiday. He had Mahler installed in a clinic straight away, and a serum treatment was begun. Everyone knew what was going on. Ever since Mahler had returned to Europe the *Neue Freie Presse* had been publishing day by day details of the condition of the patient and the treatment he was receiving.

Justi arrived, and Bruno Walter. Alma assumed that the treatment would be a long one, and wrote at the end of April to Walter Gropius suggesting that he should come to Paris. She dreamt of his 'dear, hot, and so tender hands', and asked him to send his reply care of Anna Moll. We do not know whether he came. In another letter she thanked him for the photo he had sent her, 'you whom I love before all, hold me close, as your beloved I kiss your hands'.

At the beginning of May, after a temporary improvement, Mahler's condition deteriorated. Another doctor, Professor Chvotsek, was summoned from Trieste. He persuaded Mahler that he could cure him, but only if he could move him to Vienna. 'Don't give up,' he said, 'there's no reason to do that. You've simply been working too hard.'

Mahler plucked up courage again. Meanwhile Chvotsek warned Alma that there was no hope. Mahler was put in the train to Vienna, and taken straight to hospital there. His sufferings were over. On 18 May 1911 he passed peacefully away. He was 51 years old. The Tenth Symphony would remain unfinished.

Alma gave no outward sign of sorrow or pain, but those three months of struggle with death had exhausted her. Her mother led her away. The doctors decided to keep her under supervision for a few days, and forbade her to attend her husband's funeral. She obeyed. This protective attitude to feminine fragility would be a matter for surprise nowadays. But attitudes were different then.

Carl Moll watched over the mortal remains. Mahler had demanded that his heart be pierced. That was done. He had wanted a funeral without speeches or music. In the little cemetery in Grinzing, where he was buried according to his wish next to his daughter Putzi, Vienna gave him a sumptuous funeral. Everyone was there, his friends, his enemies, the curious crowd. Heaps of flowers surrounded the grave. It rained. A priest blessed the coffin. It was all over.

As usual those who had been his bitterest critics now praised the stricken genius and covered him with flowers in every sense of the term. The press was given over to funeral orations. Berta Zuckerkandl, who stayed away from the ceremony to show her scorn of convention, was sickened by it all. She was wrong. The living are afraid of the dead and so they never fail to speak well of those who have just passed on. Even Karl Kraus joined in.

Half a century later people would say and write and repeat that Alma killed Mahler, that she had so affected his state of mind that the illness had caught him with his defences down, unable to resist. A somewhat far-fetched theory, considering that Mahler's illness was due to an infection. Penicillin would probably have saved him. But if it is true that one can die of love, then yes, that is what he died of.

8. 'Alma Oskar Kokoschka'

So Alma was now alone at her mother's house on the Hohe Warte, delivered certainly, but also bereft. For a long time to come Mahler would be present in her dreams, in her thoughts, in her diary, as she pondered on the meaning of life. Bereft then, but freed.

The young widow of 31, soon to be 32, not in mourning in compliance with the wishes of the departed, was well provided for. The Opera paid her a pension, Mahler had left 100,000 dollars in New York in her name and 139,000 crowns in Vienna, plus the piece of land on the Semmering. It was not a fortune, but she was comfortably off. For six months, in deference to convention, she would not be seen in society. And then, in the city still intoxicated with culture, festivals, and art, a new figure would appear on the scene: Mahler's widow.

The deference, the homage—now that we know Alma a little, we can imagine how she would enjoy it all. What is more, this woman so richly endowed with seductive power would now have an added aura, she would be marked with the seal of the great man, the final touch that would make her irresistible.

Gropius came post haste. He was himself grieving over the death of his father, to whom he had been much attached. Their reunion was an occasion for emotion, tears, and the rediscovery of the desire they felt for each other and which was as strong as ever. They had not met for several months and had a million things to say to each other. Since nothing now stood in their way, the moment had come to take stock of their feelings for each other, their future relationship, and the marriage that Gropius so ardently desired.

Then, in the hotel room where they were lying side by side, happy and relaxed, Alma behaved again in the curious way we have already seen. Plied with questions by her lover, instead of simply taking refuge in a white lie, she said yes, yes, during all those months she had made love with Mahler when he had wanted it, yes, she had given him all the tenderness he needed, yes.

She could never tell a lie, Alma, though whether out of pride in herself or to provoke a scene it is impossible to say. Gropius took this confession very badly. He felt fooled, deceived, and betrayed. When she left him, he wrote to her: 'One important question which you must answer, please. When did you first let him make love to you again?' What a genius lovers have for torturing themselves!

When he left Vienna, gnawed with doubt, in mid-August 1911, to return to Berlin where he had work to do, the climate between them had deteriorated. Goodbye for ever was in the air. She panicked and wrote to him that it would be stupid to end things like that and he replied. They continued to write to each other. And since Gropius had the strange habit of keeping copies of his love-letters, we can observe that while he was reluctant to break with Alma, he neverthe-less made the attempt, claiming that health reasons justified his refusal to come and join her in Paris, where she had a flat at her disposal. All the signs were that this German love affair was coming unstuck. But we shall see that it was not as easy as that to fall out of love with Alma.

In the mean time, a new suitor had emerged: the good Doctor Fraenkel from New York. He too wanted to marry her. Of Viennese origin, he courted her in German. She agreed to go with him on a cruise to Corfu—a splendid display of freedom in the face of the prejudices of the time. He was droll, quick-witted, full of ideas. 'Prometheus didn't give mankind fire for them to make matches with', he said. This entertaining character had only one handicap: she didn't want him. But of the voyage she was to keep one memory. One day an Albanian minister had come on board, and in conversation he had quoted a proverb of his country: 'It is not the assassin who is guilty, it is his victim.' A motto for Alma, as it were. She would never forget it.

In the autumn she left the Molls' house and moved with her daughter to Elisabethenstrasse. It was the first time she had been free to furnish an interior as she wished. In the Auenbruggergasse, and then at Maiernigg, she had always moved in among Mahler's furniture. It pleased her therefore to be able this time to arrange the new home in the purest Secessionist style, with a red music room in which she could seat eighty people when she played the hostess in her gold lamé dress.

Six months after Mahler's death she appeared for the first time in public, in Munich where Bruno Walter was conducting *The Song of the Earth*. She didn't really like Bruno Walter, she had always been jealous of his intimacy with Mahler. When, later, Walter published his book on Mahler she was furious: 'There isn't a word about me in it . . . They still hate me, just because I'm a pure, beautiful Christian!' But during the concert in Munich she gracefully acknowledged the homage paid to her, and played for the first time the role she would henceforth play so often, that of the widow of the great man.

In the train which took her back to Vienna she met someone she had already come across, Paul Kammerer, biologist and music-lover. And guess what happened! He fell doubly in love, with Alma and with Mahler's ghost. He was married, but found an excellent excuse for seeing Alma: he persuaded her to come and work in his laboratory. Which she did, not without interest, while letting him adore her. He saw her every day, but also wrote her never-ending letters.

In particular he wrote this: 'I know that each of my meetings with Alma Mahler gives me renewed energy for my work. When I am with her, I garner the energy I need to be productive.' That was the marvellous thing about Alma. Others might be more beautiful, more intelligent, or otherwise better than she was. But she had the gift of replenishing her lovers' fuel supply.

He was soon on first-name terms with her, calling her 'my beloved Alma', threatening, if she did not respond to his love, to commit suicide on Mahler's grave. She confided to him that she was thinking of marrying again, without saying to whom, but at the same time was wondering whether the man she was thinking of would be capable of 'belonging to her'.

In January 1912 she rejoined Gropius in Berlin where, suddenly, everything displeased her. The city first of all, but that was a minor matter. Then there was Gropius's attitude to her. He insisted on introducing Alma to his mother and sister, and showed himself to be a tender and attentive son, which exasperated the jealous Alma. Frau Gropius was an upper middle-class Prussian whose manners, background, and tone were foreign to Alma. Alma herself appeared in these surroundings not with the halo she wore in Vienna but as an exotic personage suspected of having turned the head of the son of the house, who was four years younger than herself.

The two women disliked each other from the start and sparks flew. Feeling that she was being judged unfavourably, Alma became aggressive. She had behaved in the same way earlier when Mahler presented her to his friends. Nose in the air, she declared that she detested the 'narrow-mindedness' of the Gropius family. Frau Gropius and her daughter displayed icy disapproval . . .

After that visit, Alma's letters to Gropius remained unanswered, until one day he informed her: 'No, things can never be the same as before. Everything has changed fundamentally.' They continued to correspond, but without much enthusiasm. She was alone therefore, undecided about Walter Gropius, when Carl Moll introduced her to a young painter, whom he had invited for a meal with them. His name was Oskar Kokoschka. He was 24 years old, and had already provided the gossips with much to talk about.

He was tall, unprepossessing to say the least, his appearance dominated by obliquely set eyes, ears which stuck out, and red hands, but with an air of unconcern that gave him a certain elegance. He was a strange fellow. He boasted that he had inherited the gift of second sight from his mother and grandmother. He used to say that, when he painted a portrait, 'It's as though I'm using a tin-opener to bring to light a personality hitherto shut in by convention.' There was something in it. Unfortunately, he was not getting many commissions. His brutal, violent style of painting was intimidating. His pictures were a far cry from the insidious graces of Klimt.

Born in Pöchlarn, Lower Austria, Kokoschka had grown up in poverty in the suburbs of Vienna. He could recite Shakespeare by heart. He was violent and rowdy, a rebel by nature. At the Vienna School of Arts and Crafts, then the most progressive of the art schools, where he studied to become an art teacher, he drew out a knife which had belonged to his grandfather, and threatened to commit suicide if he was not awarded the scholarship which one of his teachers wanted to withhold from him on the grounds that he was a trouble-maker. Another teacher came to his rescue by affirming that 'he was a born artist'.

In the summer of 1908 a large international exhibition was organized by the Wiener Werkstätten, in conjunction with the Vienna School of Arts and Crafts and the group of artists who had followed Klimt when the Secessionists had split up. The exhibition (*Kunstschau*) was part of the emperor's jubilee celebrations, a programme of festivities to which the whole city was given over. The government had granted the organizers of the Kunstschau a subsidy of 30,000 crowns and provided them with an enormous exhibition site on which Josef Hoffmann erected forty-five pavilions surrounded by terraces and gardens.

Klimt displayed sixteen superb canvases. A large contribution by contemporary artists—Gauguin, Bonnard, Matisse, Vlaminck, Vuillard, Van Gogh—hung on the line. All the famous names were there, competition for space was keen. On the recommendation of his teachers Kokoschka was allocated a small room. A jury, chaired by Klimt, had to judge whether the pictures were worthy of display. But Kokoschka would not let them in.

'I won't open the door', he said, 'until I've been given a guarantee that my work will be shown to the public.' 'Let the lad get himself torn to bits by the press if he wants to', said Klimt, and passed on. Kokoschka exhibited among other things a series of designs for tapestry entitled *The Dream Bearers*, and a bust in coloured clay, *The Warrior*, a self-portrait, open-mouthed, shouting defiance.

The press called him 'chief of the savages', 'a Gauguin gone mad', and referred to his room at the exhibition as 'the chamber of horrors'. But one collector declared him to be 'the smash hit of the Exhibition' and purchased *The Dream Bearers*. The architect Adolf Loos bought *The Warrior*, and later became the young painter's best friend.

The following year an open-air theatre was set up in the Kunstschau gardens for the performance of ballets and concerts. Kokoschka, who had written a play entitled *Murderer, Hope of Women*, got permission to have it put on there. He was also authorized to advertise the performance by poster. The poster he produced—a red man lying in the bosom of a white woman (red the colour of life, white the colour of death)—has since become a classic. There is scarcely a book on Kokoschka or on the art of that period that does not show it, often it is in pride of place on the outside cover. It became the symbol of what later became known as 'expressionism'. The play was a resounding failure. The audience protested. The actors read out a defiant justification written by the author. The public, scandalized, passed from verbal to physical abuse. Fighting broke out. Loos and Karl Kraus, who were in the audience, notified the authorities and a squad of policemen was sent to restore order. The next day the press was merciless. Kokoschka was 'a degenerate artist', 'a corrupter of youth', 'a gallows-bird'.

'I couldn't afford to go to the theatre, so I decided to put on my own play', said Kokoschka. The Minister for Education got the director of the School of Arts and Crafts (none other than Alfred Roller, the man whom Mahler employed to design his opera sets) to deprive Kokoschka of his scholarship grant. Kokoschka riposted by appearing with clean-shaven skull so that people would know 'that I am a man marked by destiny'. In order to eat, he took his drawings along to the Café Central and hawked them from table to table. He was then 22.

Fortunately Loos was at hand. The architect, his reputation well-established, was twenty-five years older than Kokoschka. He helped the painter to obtain orders for portraits, and introduced him to a stimulating intellectual milieu which was quite new to him. Loos had taken part in the Secession from its earliest days, but had soon distanced himself from excessive ornamentation, the transformation of houses and interiors into objects of art, and the exaggerated use of accessories, in a word, 'aestheticism'. Just as his friend Karl Kraus wanted to purge language of all pretentiousness which stood in the way of clarity of thought, so Loos wanted to purify architecture, the environment, the city, and even the clothes people wore, and make them more rational.

Kokoschka became a passionate advocate and practitioner of 'the psychological portrait' in which, he said, the life force emanating from the model was captured by the artist and expressed on his canvas. Through Loos he got to know Karl Kraus. The journalist slept by day and worked by night after dining in his favourite café. Kokoschka enjoyed the rare privilege of sitting with the select few at his table, and giving his opinion on this or that article which had been or was about to be published in *Die Fackel.* He did a striking portrait of Kraus, young, lively, and sharp-eyed.

Another crusader for austerity of style was the musician Arnold Schönberg. In 1911 the performance of one of his atonal pieces provoked such a riot that an ambulance had to be called. Then there was Egon Schiele, like Kokoschka a protégé of Loos, but also of Klimt. He too belonged to the expressionist movement. At the age of 22 he was condemned to twenty-four days in prison for some amateurish pornographic drawings.

These young artists were already sounding the death-knell of Viennese aestheticism, and raising questions about the social function of art. But Vienna closed its eyes and ears to them, as it did to Freud, whose ideas had only found acceptance among a few writers, in particular Hofmannsthal and Schnitzler.

'We must rise above this pampered way of life which is stultifying us', wrote Hofmannsthal. 'The life we lead is not good. Intellectually we are living like kept women on a diet of French salads and sorbets.' The novelist Robert Musil wrote later: 'Austria had a smiling face simply because it had no facial muscles left.'

In 1911 a group of painters, the Hagenbund, organized an exhibition. Kokoschka's pictures figured prominently. At the private viewing before it opened to the public, there was a sudden stir among the official personalities present, and Archduke Franz Ferdinand, the Crown Prince, appeared. He passed the pictures in review, examining them in silence one by one, then took up a position in the middle of the room, and shouted: 'Pig's muck!' Three steps forward: 'Pig's muck!' again. Then, pointing to one of Kokoschka's pictures: 'Somebody should break every bone in that man's body.' Shortly afterwards it was announced that the exhibition was to be forbidden by order of the Crown Prince. But the emperor intervened to prevent things going that far.

That then was the young painter whom Carl Moll, on Adolf Loos's suggestion, had commissioned to paint his portrait, and whom he had invited to lunch, with his daughter-in-law, at his lovely Hohe Warte house which Hoffmann had decorated. The accounts given by Alma and Kokoschka of this first encounter cannot be easily reconciled.

According to Alma, he was wearing a threadbare suit and down-at-heel shoes, and the handkerchief he held in front of his mouth when he coughed was stained with blood. He had brought coarse-grained paper with him to make a drawing of her, and she sat for him for a while and then went to the piano ... The next thing she knew he had flung his arms around her in a passionate embrace. She remained ice-cool, she says, and freed herself at once.

According to Kokoschka, however, he was elegantly dressed in accordance with the recommendation of his friend Loos, whose sartorial model was the English gentleman. And if the two men were well-dressed, it was because Loos decorated the shops of the best tailors in Vienna, including the tailor to the Court, while Kokoschka did their portraits and got well-cut suits in exchange.

As for what happened subsequently, if Kokoschka is to be believed, Alma led him imperiously into the next room where there was a piano, and there sang—for him alone, she told him—'The Death of Isolde'. 'I was fascinated by the sight of her,' he says, 'young, moving in her mourning, because she was so beautiful and so lovely.'

And he goes on:

When she suggested that I should paint her, at her home, I was both happy and worried. In the first place I had never before painted a woman who seemed to have fallen in love with me at first sight, and furthermore I was a bit scared. How could a fellow expect to be happy stepping into the shoes of a man who had died just before?

In short, the sudden embrace had been provoked by Alma.

Whatever the facts, the next day Alma received a letter from Kokoschka, the first of many. He came straight to the point: '[If you can have respect for me, and want to be as pure as you were yesterday] make a real sacrifice for me and become my wife, in secret so long as I am poor.'

No trace of Kokoschka being scared there: to become his wife. He had known her for twenty-four hours. And he added: 'You will have to look after me until I can really be for you the one who doesn't drag you down, but lifts you up. Since you asked me yesterday to do that, I believed in you as I never believed [in] anyone but myself.'

What was it she had asked him to do? Not to rape her on the piano, apparently. 'I only wanted peace and concentration', wrote Alma, describing this period of her life, thus effectively putting paid to any credibility she might claim for her autobiography. By way of 'peace and concentration', she flung herself into a passionate affair of her own choosing which she pursued recklessly, transgressing all the conventions of the time.

She was now 32, Kokoschka 25. They were going to be swept along on a huge, long-lasting surge of physical passion. When he wasn't making love to her, he painted her, one picture after another. He was possessive, exacting, and jealous. He lived in the city in a little studio flat with walls painted black. There he made her pose for him for endless hours.

Sometimes it was he who went to her. Her house had a garden. When he left her late at night he would prowl up and down beneath her window until three or four in the morning to make sure she did not receive further visitors. They quarrelled, violently. Afterwards he would return crestfallen and carrying armfuls of flowers which he would strew over the bed. She was convinced of his talent, his genius even, and had decided that, since she had the resources to do so, she would give him material assistance until he gained the recognition he deserved. On their frequent journeys together she bought the train tickets and paid the hotel bills. This was the better Alma, the one for whom art was a supreme value, the creative artist sacred.

The other Alma took and kept Oskar away from Adolf Loos, who disapproved of their affair, but she did not surround him with other friends in compensation. Admittedly, he was a difficult animal to get on with. Here is one example of the kind of letters he wrote to her: 'Alma. I happened to be passing by your house at about ten o'clock, and could have wept for anger that you go on surrounding yourself with satellites while leaving me to skulk in the shadows. I warn you now to make up your mind whether you want to take me or leave me. I would have loved you extraordinarily much.' He signed with a combination of their two names (Alma Oskar Kokoschka) as if to indicate that they were now one.

In 1912 Alma went on a trip to Paris with a friend, Lili Leiser. She had few women friends, and Lili was a rather special one in that, besides being ostentatiously rich, she was a lesbian. But there is nothing to indicate that Alma had any leanings in that direction.

Oskar wrote to her every day, begging her to marry him: 'Be for ever one and indivisible with me together in eternal happiness.' If all

Alma's men were so keen to marry her, it was no doubt because they loved her, but also because marriage was a way of exorcizing Mahler. Oskar's devouring passion was transmuted into religious adoration, his jealousy into obsession. Alma became, in his eyes, the incarnation of 'the eternal feminine', as Goethe put it. And when the pleasure of the senses brought religious adoration with it, Alma liked it. Who wouldn't?

They spent a few weeks in Naples together. 'A period of fullness and richness', wrote Alma. It seems as if, then, she completely accepted her feminine role, as one who found fulfilment in love rather than in her own achievements. Her ambitions provisionally set aside, her narcissism fully satisfied by Oskar's ceaseless paintings of her, drowsy with sensual pleasure, she was at peace with herself and the world.

In all passionate affairs there are these short lulls when the conflicting forces in each of the partners are stilled, when the colour of the sky and the mood of the lovers are in harmonious conjunction, and the twofold urge of each for the other is in perfect balance. When that happens, they are happy beyond words. But for women such moments are often tinged with sadness, because they are afraid, afraid of the time when the idyll must end. The sturdy manly element in Alma's make-up protected her against such fears. She was not one of those women who ask: 'Will you always love me?' She took that for granted.

Their Italian journey (for Kokoschka a very productive period) came to an end. Alma had to return home. Gucki was waiting for her mother to take her to the seaside, in Holland. Lili Leiser would accompany them. They had hardly said goodbye to each other before Oskar began to complain. 'Alma, I just can't grasp the fact that I shan't be able to see you for weeks. I'm not used to having an external difficulty hold me back'.

What was her reply? His next letter contained the following lines: 'I'm absolutely shattered that you could think me such an idiot as to begrudge you your holiday. Would you have said such a thing to your first husband? How can you take the slightest notice of what that Jewish, free-thinking crowd around you say, when you know for certain that I am only thinking the best for you?'

The 'Jewish crowd' around Alma must have begun to find her affair with Oskar a bit too engrossing. The Molls, on the other hand, had taken him to their hearts. During that summer Alma, torn between the pressing attentions of Lili Leiser and the ardent supplications of Kokoschka, decided in favour of the latter, and rejoined him in Munich. They then went on to Mürren, in Switzerland. There she posed for him, sitting on the hotel balcony. And then abruptly, she went away again. Lili Leiser was left to take Gucki back to Vienna.

Alma was pregnant and went into a clinic for an abortion. Then for some weeks she complained of ill health, and made that an excuse for keeping Oskar at a distance. But could Oskar be kept at a distance? And did she want this? Evidently not, since she decided to have a house built on the plot of land on the Semmering, and to live there with him. Oskar took part in discussions with Carl Moll on the plans for the house. It was to be relatively small, eight rooms. The surrounding countryside was superb. And from Vienna it was possible to go by train to the Semmering and back in one day.

Lili Leiser, who certainly had as much perseverance as Kokoschka if not the same arguments, tried to buy a neighbouring plot of land, but it seems that her project ultimately fell through.

Oskar then behaved like a madman. While Alma was away taking a cure at Franzenbad, he searched through her papers, found her birth certificate, and used it to order the banns for their marriage to be published. She returned, exploded, insulted him, and punished him: thenceforth they would only see each other once every three days.

During all this period, Alma's correspondence with Walter Gropius had continued without interruption. She had never told him about Kokoschka, of course. But rumours may have reached his ears. In any case, in the spring of 1913 Gropius recognized Alma in one of Kokoschka's pictures, a double portrait of Alma and him exhibited in Berlin. And this time Gropius wrote a letter breaking it off, finally and irrevocably. Alma greeted the decision with seeming indifference. She was totally absorbed in her passion for Kokoschka.

In August she took him to the Dolomites, where she rested while he worked. Where was the Alma we formerly knew, the ravaged creature whose diary was one long record of sorrows? Now that her carnal needs were being satisfied by a man whose talent impressed her, she had calmed down. 'I found once more the inner harmony I had possessed as a child without knowing it', she wrote. 'The earth offers us the purest happiness, we just don't see it, we are too full of our own importance . . . The most important ideas are deep down in the unconscious—and in our upper consciousness a growing thing can't be perceived or understood. The unconscious is the fire of the world!'

Those were sentiments that would have pleased Doctor Freud. In spite of all the good doctor had done for Mahler, Alma always ran him down: 'He's an idiot'. The bill he had sent her for services rendered, after his patient-for-one-day had died, still rankled.

So Alma was fine, letting herself be loved. It was Kokoschka's turn to feel there was something wrong, aware as he was of his dependence on her. He tried to free himself. It was just another of those occasions when they separated only to reunite more closely than before.

But Oskar's mother now came on the scene. She hated Alma, 'that society woman' who, she believed, was ruining her son's future, and wrote to her, straight out: 'If you see Oskar again, I'll shoot you.' Frau Gropius would never have said anything like that, but both women had the same unerring instinct mothers have about other women who are doing harm to their sons. The fact was that Alma was not exactly the type of woman to make an ideal daughter-in-law.

One morning Frau Kokoschka was there at Alma's gate, with Alma watching her through her half-open window. Oskar came up, saw his mother pacing up and down with her hand in her coat pocket grasping something that could well have been a dangerous weapon. It turned out to be just a piece of wood. He took her home. And came back to his imprisonment.

At the Vienna Festival of 1912 Bruno Walter conducted the world première of Mahler's Ninth Symphony. Alma was there, of course. She asked Kokoschka to be there too. The very idea made him squirm.

Alma, I can't come to peace in you so long as I know that there's someone else, whether dead or alive, in you. Why have you invited me to a dance of death and want me to spend hours silently watching while you, a spiritual slave, bow to the rhythm of the man who was and must be a stranger to you? I can't see you on the day you have chosen to remember this man because I can never reconcile myself to that rigid complex of feelings in you which is so utterly foreign to me.

You must start a completely new life with me, a girl's life (*Mädchenleben*), if we are to be happy and for ever one, Alma.

But Alma had no intention of banishing Mahler's ghost, quite the contrary. She clearly wanted to play her part to enhance her power of attraction. What jealousy could be more tantalizing than that inspired by a man who was dead?

Oskar wrote her letter after letter, complaining, beseeching. 'If you don't soon become my wife my great talent will come to a miserable end. You must revive me at night like a magic potion . . . I don't need to take you away from your set of friends in the daytime, I can work all day and give out what I have absorbed at night'. Again this idea of Alma as the creative artist's energy supply!

'Alma, believe me, you are the woman and I am the artist . . . and how we seek each other, want each other, must have each other so that destiny . . . can be fulfilled. You give life to useless people. Destiny meant you for me, will you deprive me of that?' Alma found a good reply. 'I'll marry you', she told him, 'when you have produced a masterpiece.'

The extraordinary thing is that he did it—he produced the masterpiece! The picture, which hangs today in the museum in Basle, is entitled *Die Windsbraut* (in English called 'The Tempest'). It shows a couple lying in an enormous cockle-shell in the midst of a raging sea. The woman, Alma, hair loose, is resting her head peacefully on the man's shoulder. The man, a tortured look in his eyes, is Kokoschka.

While he was working on the picture Alma kept up the idea of a barter, a wedding for a masterpiece. But at the beginning of 1914 she went off to Paris again. She was a restless soul and could never stay long in the same place. Oskar got worried: 'If you really want to become my wife', he wrote, 'you'll have to get used to obeying me occasionally. Alma, don't spend money on me. You know I don't like luxuries, it's not in my nature.' She sent him a present all the same, which he received without pleasure. 'Our heaven is the same,' he told her, 'but our worlds are different.'

The *Windsbraut* bears the date 1914. It was finished at the same time as the house on the Semmering in which they were to live together. Once again Alma was pregnant, but this time happy to be so, it seems. Kokoschka, overjoyed, took this as an assurance that they would shortly be married. While everyone—Alma, Anna Moll, the servants—was busy with the moving-in, hanging up curtains, sorting out books, installing the kitchen, Oskar was painting a fresco over the fireplace in the living-room. It showed Alma, surrounded by flames, rising up to paradise, leaving Oskar below, in hell, surrounded by serpents.

Suddenly, in the midst of this happy domesticity, the postman arrived with a parcel. It was Mahler's death-mask. Kokoschka began to shout. He wouldn't tolerate anything in the house that would be a permanent reminder of Alma's past. Alma calmly set up the mask in an appropriate place. He raved. She insisted. He said horrible things. She replied in kind. People have rows about all sorts of things. But that one shook them both profoundly. Some days later Alma went to the clinic for an abortion. Oskar could not get over it.

'So, that too seems to be over,' wrote Alma on 17 May 1914, 'something that I thought would last.' Things between them became chaotic, tense, and bitter, but they had still not managed to make the final break when, on 28 June, the grave news broke: Archduke Ferdinand and his wife had been assassinated at Sarajevo. There is nothing to indicate that Alma had the slightest apprehension of what this news might mean, nor even that she bothered to think about it at all. As a general rule she couldn't care less what happened in the outside world.

The day Austria declared war on Serbia she was at home on the Semmering, and wrote in her diary:

[I am] perfectly calm and peaceful here, and that's exactly how I wanted it to be . . . He fulfilled my life and destroyed it at the same time. I don't know where I shall go now. Why, oh why did I abandon the peaceful crowd for a fiery blast-furnace? But do I still love this man? Or do I already hate him? Why am I so worried?

And when she heard on the radio of the declaration of war, she wrote this priceless comment: 'I sometimes imagine that I'm the one who has caused this whole upheaval . . . '.

Kokoschka was working in his studio when he heard the newspaper boys shouting about a special edition. He went down to the café to find out what was happening. His first reaction was to think: 'I'm 28, why wait until I'm called up? I'll volunteer.' But he left it until the following January before he enlisted.

Meanwhle his relations with Alma grew worse and worse. She had had enough, that was clear. She sent him money because she knew he was hard up, and that irritated him. He wanted her at all costs to get her papers in order so that she could take refuge in Switzerland, something she had no intention of doing. In spite of everything, she must still have felt something for Kokoschka. When they were in Vienna he spent the night at her home, and the rest of the time they lived together on the Semmering. But for Alma the time for love, when Oskar filled her world, was over.

A few days after her thirty-fifth birthday, in August 1914, she wrote: 'I'd like to get away from Oskar. He doesn't fit in with my life any more. He takes my drive away from me . . . We must bring things to an end. But I still like him so much—too much!' There follow some thoughts about music! 'But I know now that I can never sing again except in death. I shall never again be slave to a man, because in future I shall only worry about my own well-being and the achievement of my ambitions.' 'Achievement', the old refrain, comes back like a throbbing pain whenever she is in crisis. For three years there had not been a word about it.

A little while later: 'I would like to find another man, but one who would go away, disappear from my life, before everything collapses. Yesterday evening I ran away from Oskar.' That is to say, she had gone with Lili Leiser to spend the evening with the collector, Karl Reininghaus. There she had met friends, Klimt and an archaeologist. With those two 'I gossiped until three in the morning. I was almost happy that night—after the long isolation of recent years with Oskar Kokoschka. That evening was like a cure for me.' Typical for someone emerging from a love affair. From now on she would rarely complain of being lonely.

As usual, there was no lack of suitors. The first was the insufferable Hans Pfitzner, who had come to Vienna for the rehearsals of his opera *Palestrina*. One day he stood before her door, with his luggage. He raised his hands in horror when he caught sight of the picture Kokoschka had painted of her. He thought it hideous. Then, on the sofa, he threw his arms around her. But she just laughed, and he gave up, crestfallen, saying she had led him on. No doubt he was right. He continued to be a frequent visitor, but made no further attempts to get close.

Kokoschka, on the other hand, didn't give up. And Alma couldn't decide whether to keep him or get rid of him. They spent New Year's Eve together, and Oskar wrote later to her: 'the way you drew me into your bed again, you were unforgettably beautiful, unforgettably sublime'. At the same time she kept on at him to volunteer before he was called up, and suddenly he could stand it no longer, and enlisted. The infantry turned him down, because his constitution was too weak. The artillery turned him down, because his grasp of mathematics was too weak. Finally Loos—good old Loos—managed to get him into the cavalry, a branch of the Dual Monarchy's armed forces which enjoyed great prestige. Loos was not sorry to get him away from Alma. He had had to put up with her hostility for all those years.

But a cavalryman had to report complete with his horse. Oskar raised the necessary cash by selling the *Windsbraut* to a Hamburg pharmacist. Then his mother and Loos went to a horse dealer and bought a mare. There remained the uniform. It was made to measure for him by one of the tailors who liked paintings.

At last Oskar went off, after Alma had kissed him somewhat absent-mindedly goodbye. As he was taking leave of his mother he handed her a necklace of red pearls, a present from Alma, and asked her to keep it as a reminder of his love. What was Alma thinking of as her lover went off to war (and not just any war, the dead were already legion)? She was wondering how she could get hold of Walter Gropius again.

In January she had learnt that Gropius, called up at the start of hostilities, had been wounded. She wrote to him and he replied. And her diary entry for 2 February 1915 read: 'I have the feeling that Gropius doesn't love me any more. He sees me as another woman. I would have to do a lot of things to prepare myself to be still available in his eyes ... This German would not be unfaithful to me like Oskar Kokoschka.' And she concluded: 'It won't take me long to win him over.' She was right.

Accompanied by Lili Leiser, she arrived in Berlin. At first things did not go as easily as she had thought. Of her efforts to win Gropius back she wrote: 'I came to Berlin with the shameful intention of getting back together with this upper-class son of the muses.' The days were spent 'in tearful questioning, the nights in tearful answers. Walter Gropius can't get over my affair with Oskar Kokoschka'.

But on the last evening they went to a restaurant, they had a drink or two, they were sad at the thought that they would soon be going their separate ways. Before going back to the front, Gropius wanted to visit his mother in Hanover. Alma went with him to the station. And there he clung to her so closely that when the train moved off she had to climb up into the carriage with him. 'Without a nightdress or any of the usual necessaries, I had become this man's booty. I must say I enjoyed it.'

The next day she returned to Berlin, where Lili Leiser was waiting for her, still hoping that on one of their journeys together Alma would one night be tempted to taste pleasures more subtle than a man's embraces. Together they went to see Schönberg, who was now living in a Berlin suburb. The young man was finding it hard to make ends meet.

Alma had promised Mahler that she would look after Schönberg. As a general rule, she was always resourceful and generous when it came to helping young musicians. It was she who had Alban Berg's *Wozzeck* published. He dedicated the score to her. She had also seen to it that Schönberg got the prize awarded by the Gustav Mahler Foundation. This time she suggested organizing a concert in Vienna, at which he would conduct Beethoven's Ninth Symphony in Mahler's orchestration. The concert duly took place. The hall was almost empty. Schönberg received his honorarium. Alma paid off the deficit.

Before leaving Berlin she saw Gropius again. He looked very handsome in his lieutenant's uniform. 'He suddenly began to behave like a husband—he did everything he could to get me to marry him, and I am still trembling at the idea that it might actually happen', she wrote, on her return home. What did she really want? She had decided that it wouldn't take her long to 'win over this German', she now had him in her clutches, and was delighted at her victory. But she didn't love him, not any more, if she had ever loved him. She wanted him because he was so Aryan, but his real stature escaped her.

Commenting in her diary on a letter Gropius had sent her from the front, and in which he expressed once again his jealousy of

Kokoschka, she wrote: 'Oskar has a right to be inconsiderate, but not this man, not this little, ordinary man.' An ordinary man, Walter Gropius? She knew better than that. But as far as art was concerned, they didn't speak the same language. When she told him how beautiful the New York skyscrapers were, he wasn't interested. And when he explained to her that it was time to have done with art for art's sake, that architecture and artistic creation must be rooted in social reality, he might as well have been talking Chinese. She was a Viennese woman of her time, deaf to the threatening rumblings of the world. He was a man of the future.

With her two lovers at the front, she was alone once more. She took up composition again, and reworked four of her Lieder. But Mahler's publisher was not interested, and she lost heart. If at that moment in her life she had had a Zemlinsky to make her work, stimulate her, and give her renewed confidence in her abilities, she might perhaps have found the strength to create, the necessary tenacity . . . Instead of which she went off to do a cure at Franzenbad, and replied to the letters which Oskar and Gropius sent her from whatever military encampment they might be in.

'I love you and am holding on to you, whatever you think, whoever you are and wherever you are', wrote Kokoschka. That was not Gropius's style. But it was Gropius who won the day. On 18 August 1915, Lieutenant Walter Gropius was given two days' leave to marry, in Berlin, Alma Schindler, widow of Gustav Mahler, and then he returned to the front. The wedding remained secret for the time being. Frau Gropius, who dreaded the idea that they might marry, was not informed.

A strange union! Alma was 36, he was 31, and basically they had nothing in common. On 19 August she wrote: 'On 18 August I got married to Walter Gropius. I'm home and dry. Henceforth nothing can throw me off my path. My objective is clear—simply to make this man happy. I am unshakeable, calm, stimulated as never before. God preserve my love!' Even God was to find that impossible. She saw her husband only on the few occasions when he had leave, but enjoyed her new status as wife and was glad to know that she was pregnant. For the seventh time. And the news transformed her relations with her mother-in-law.

Frau Gropius, full of tender concern, came to the Semmering.

She now saw Alma in a new light, as the woman who was carrying her son's child. Alma enjoyed playing her new role, and was at her most charming. The hatchet was tacitly buried. Frau Gropius wrote to her son: 'I admire the way Alma has succeeded in remaining so simple and childlike, in spite of the life she leads. I can't judge her maturity and intelligence because she doesn't put them on display, and that's what I like most about her.' Of all Alma's conquests, that one was possibly the most remarkable!

One day the newspapers announced that Kokoschka had died on the field of battle. Alma's reaction? She ran at once to Oskar's studio, of which she had kept the key, and took back her letters. As an afterthought she also carried away some hundreds of drawings and sketches.

But Kokoschka was by no means dead. During a skirmish with a Cossack patrol he had received a shot in the head and a bayonet wound in the chest, and had indeed been left for dead. But he was now in a hospital in Vienna, where he learnt of Alma's marriage. He begged and implored his old friend Loos to go to Alma and persuade her to come and see him. Loos must have been extremely reluctant to undertake this errand, but Kokoschka was a sick man whose life hung in the balance.

Alma haughtily refused to accede to his request, and could not be moved to reconsider her rejection, thus showing herself to be a worthy disciple of the Nietzschean philosophy Burckhard had inculcated in her and which suited her so well: 'Anyone who needs help doesn't deserve to receive it.' Kokoschka recovered, came out of hospital, went at once to his mother's and asked her for the red necklace he had asked her to keep for him. Frau Kokoschka took up a pot of flowers, dashed it to the ground, and picked out the necklace from among the fragments. Kokoschka saw a message in that: he had lost Alma.

He went back to his regiment. He was badly wounded again, this time in Hungary, when a bridge was blown up under him. And again he came back to a hospital in Vienna, and recovered. One day, at a concert, Loos caught sight of Alma and spoke to her. What was she waiting for to go and see Oskar? Without her he would be finished. He was no longer working. He was in no condition to do so. She had a duty to see him.

But of duties towards creative artists who were stupid enough to love her Alma had had more than enough. In her diary she wrote: 'Oskar Kokoschka has become a strange shadow for me—I have no further interest in how he lives. And yet I loved him!' `

And what about him? For the remainder of his life he kept sending her strange reminders of his continued existence. He wrote letters, sent her telegrams, flowers, an invitation to his play *Orpheus and Eurydice* which was being performed in Frankfurt. One day he caught sight of her in Venice where he was exhibiting in the 1922 Biennale, and arranged to meet her the next morning at the Café Florian. But he failed to turn up. He sent her sibylline messages, imperious postcards.

'For a few years it gave me pleasure—perhaps it was inexcusable—to rake around in the ashes of a passion grown cold . . .' The most spectacular of his gestures took place in Dresden. He had been working for a long time in Germany, because he didn't want to stay any more in the same town as Alma. In Dresden he lived on the first floor of a summer-house. He ordered a doll from a craftswoman. It was to be life-size, in cloth and woodwork, and would be a faithful reproduction of Alma's body and head. He supervised the work down to the last detail. While waiting for the doll to be delivered, he bought Parisian underclothes and frocks in which to dress it. Two men finally appeared carrying a huge box. The doll was inside, lying on wood-shavings. When Kokoschka's manservant saw his master with the doll, he fainted with shock. When he had recovered, he gave notice.

Helped by a maidservant, Reserl, Kokoschka dressed the doll, and christened it 'the silent woman'. Reserl was then instructed to spread rumours in the town about the charm and the mysterious origins of 'the silent woman', and how when the weather was fine, Oskar would take her for rides in a carriage, and hire a box to show her off at the Opera.

The time came to put an end to the existence of this strange companion. Oskar sent out invitations, ordered a chamber orchestra from the Opera, and installed it in the basin of the baroque fountain in the garden. Torches were lit, wine flowed copiously, the night was warm, the guests were fascinated by the 'silent woman' whom Reserl paraded up and down like a mannequin.

The drinking degenerated into an orgy. Alma's effigy, plentifully bespattered with red wine, had its head knocked off. The next day the police came to collect the corpse. Kokoschka showed them the doll, lying in the garden, decapitated. 'The garbage disposal men came in the grey light of dawn to remove the dream of Eurydice's return.'

The last letter Alma received from him was on the occasion of her seventieth birthday, in New York. He had now become famous. He was living in Switzerland. He had earlier emigrated to London after having been threatened by the Nazis, who had exhibited his paintings as examples of 'degenerate art'. His first reaction had been to put up posters in the streets of Prague demanding that Bohemia should give asylum to the child victims of Guernica. German radio had immediately threatened him: 'When we get to Prague, you'll be strung up on the nearest lamp-post.' Kokoschka didn't wait for them to arrive. He left, with his wife, thanks to a passport provided by Jan Masaryk. He lived through all the London blitz.

So, after all those troubled years, he took up his pen once more to write to Alma. The letter begins:

My dear Alma, you are still the same unruly creature, just as you were in the old days when you were mad about *Tristan and Isolde* and when you used a quill pen to scribble comments about Nietzsche in your diary, in the same rapid, unreadable handwriting that only I can understand because I know the way your mind works.

He asks her to be on the look-out for an American poet 'who knows the whole range of emotions, from tenderness to the most depraved sensuality', to translate his play *Orpheus and Eurydice*, 'so that we can tell the world what we two have done for and against each other, and pass on to posterity the living message of our love. Since the Middle Ages there has been nothing like it, for no pair of lovers has ever breathed so passionately the one through the other.'

He continues in this vein, and then concludes:

We two will still be on the stage of life when sickening banality, the trivial picture of the contemporary world, must give way to a splendour born of passion. Look at the empty and prosaic faces around you—not one of them has known the excitement of the fighter with life, of enjoyment, even of death, of laughing at the bullet in the skull, the knife in the lung. Not one, except your beloved, whom you once initiated into your secrets. Remember that this love-play is the only child we have. Take care of yourself, and try and celebrate your birthday without a hangover. Your Oskar.

Unforgettable Alma . . .

9. 'Not Guilty At All'

By September 1916 the battle for Verdun had degenerated into trench warfare of the most atrocious kind. Tens of thousands of soldiers were dying on both sides. Walter Gropius, a cavalry officer, was actively engaged on this front. But no word of any of this appears in Alma's diary.

With that admirable capacity women have of adopting a new guise for each new man in their lives, she was now playing the young wife, pregnant and respectable, snug in her house on the Semmering where, for once, she received only women, a call from Frau This, an invitation from Frau That. From time to time she jotted down nonsensical sentiments such as: 'The Jews gave us intelligence, but devoured our hearts'; or, 'Every man is priest in his own church. The woman is his parishioner who comes to pray in his church.' Just the thing for Alma!

At last, on 5 October 1916, the baby was born, a little girl whom everyone immediately adored. Alma named her Manon, after her mother-in-law. Gropius could not be there: all leave was cancelled. But he had a present sent to her, a picture by Edvard Munch, *The Midnight Sun*, which he knew she wanted. The picture was in the hands of a collector, Karl Reininghaus, a friend of theirs. Gropius asked if he might buy it. When he said why he wanted it, Reininghaus made him a present of it.

Life as a soldier's wife was decidedly not for Alma. Her affection for an absent husband slowly waned. 'I've had about enough of this makeshift existence', she wrote. 'Sometimes I get impatient and want to do something wicked. There are so many wicked things it would be nice to do. Ach! just a little bit of wickedness! My love for Walter Gropius has given way to a tired twilight-marriage. No marriage can be carried on at a distance.'

Her confinement over, she reassembled her circle of friends, Alban Berg, the Schönbergs, Klimt. Her 'salon', her Sundays in Vienna or on the Semmering, now reached out to include writers whom she tried to attract into her orbit. Arthur Schnitzler and Hofmannsthal sometimes came. It was at Alma's that Olga Schnitzler took refuge when she left her husband.

The publisher Jakob Hegner, from whom Alma had ordered ten copies of Claudel's *Tête d'or*, and who had come out of curiosity to see what a customer who would do that was like, brought along a young poet, Franz Blei. Insufferably conceited, but fascinating too, Blei was at his most brilliant one evening when Gropius was there on leave. Alma seems seriously to have considered yielding to his charms. But fate decided otherwise, and her choice fell on another poet whom Blei introduced to her.

His name was Franz Werfel. He was 27. His entry on to the Gropius family stage had a touch of vaudeville about it. In Central Europe and beyond Franz Werfel enjoyed an established reputation during his lifetime. As a novelist he rated, as we have already said, with Thomas Mann. When Blei introduced him to Alma he had already published a volume of poems, *Der Weltfreund*, which had made him an outstanding figure among the expressionist generation of the time. His poems sang the praises of brotherly love. His public readings, of his own works and those of great German poets, showed a well-developed sense of the theatre.

He was a typical Viennese, though he had been born in Prague where his father owned a large glove factory. Nonchalant, self-indulgent, talkative, he lived in cafés, chain-smoked, drank too much wine, and loved women, music (especially opera) and the pleasures of life in general. He had been called up in 1914 as a non-commissioned officer in the artillery. Whilst on home leave he had hurt himself badly jumping off a cable-railway. Court-martialled for self-inflicted wounds, he had been ordered to the Russian front. Thanks to the unsolicited intervention of a member of the aristocracy, Count Kessler, who admired his poetry—a splendid example of

Protektion in high places—he had been brought back and posted to the army press service in Vienna. It was a cushy job! He lived in the Hotel Bristol and had plenty of free time.

What else is there to say about him? He was a social democrat, which Alma found detestable. He would sometimes say: 'How can I be happy while there is still one creature on earth that suffers?', a sentiment which, Alma noted, 'I had already heard word for word from the lips of another egocentric *par excellence*, Gustav Mahler.'

There was a snag, however. He was a Jew, alas. But he was also 'a stocky little man with sensual lips, wonderful big blue eyes and a Goethean brow'. At least that was how Alma saw him. This 'stocky little' man, shorter than she was, again had some of the attributes of a father-figure for her. Others found Franz Werfel ugly, with a distressing tendency to put on weight, but full of charm. He was a brilliant and incessant talker. He knew the works of Verdi by heart and given the slightest encouragement would sing them in a fine tenor voice. He liked Mahler's music. That's a thumb-nail sketch of the young Franz Werfel.

He soon became a regular frequenter of the Gropius's household. One evening in November, when Gropius was home on leave, Alma spent 'some wonderful moments, a lovely night . . . Werfel, Blei, Gropius . . . '. They made music, they sang, 'and we were at once so intimately welded together by this our most innate element that we forgot everything around us and committed quasi musical-spiritual adultery in front of everybody. Franz Werfel is a wondrous marvel!'

A snowstorm made it impossible for the visitors to go home. Two makeshift beds were set up for them. 'I had the strangest feelings as I retired with my husband into my bedroom. Drunk with music I went to sleep by the side of someone who had become strangely foreign to me.' From then on she was to behave very badly towards her young husband. She wanted Franz, and she was going to have him. He was already hooked, but had no idea what he was letting himself in for.

At the end of 1917 the famous Dutch conductor Willem Mengelberg, who had been such an ardent supporter of Mahler, came to Vienna to give a series of concerts. Alma had the Mengelbergs to dinner and followed it by a reception to which she invited seventy people, mainly artists but also some members of the aristocracy. But she had eyes only for Franz. Three days later she went with Franz to another Mengelberg concert. He saw her home afterwards and found himself in her bedroom. The preliminaries had lasted three months in all, a long time for Alma.

'I'm crazy', she wrote, 'and so is Werfel. If I were twenty years younger I would throw everything over and go off with him. As it is I shall just have to stay weeping my heart out as I watch him go off on his darling-of-the-gods career.' The 'darling of the gods' was ten years younger than she was, and thought he was having a pleasant adventure with a married woman. It took Alma to discern in that young man anything more than a fair talent. But he was very soon to learn who it was he was dealing with. She came every day to him, in his room at the Bristol, and after they had made love she made him get down to work, something he always found difficult. And then one day he was sent to Switzerland to give lectures as part of the Austrian propaganda drive.

But Franz Werfel was a pacifist. As was his friend Berta Zucker-kandl. She, at that time, was busy organizing secret conversations with a view to contriving a separate peace between Austria and France, conversations which Clemenceau, once in power, promptly put a stop to. In Zurich, before an audience of young workers, Franz Werfel said things which scandalized the Austrian community in that city. Vienna cancelled his mission, but he persisted. He gave further lectures at Berne and Davos. 'A terrific success!' declared Berta. The *Protektion* Werfel enjoyed must have been very effective. He was simply ordered back to Vienna.

He was afraid Alma might have forgotten him. But there was little chance of that: she was pregnant again. By Werfel—at any rate, that's what she told him. As we have already seen, Alma, like the women of her time, was not too worried about resorting to abortion. But this time she had no intention of doing so.

Her husband was serving in an area too distant from Vienna to allow him to obtain home leave. So she arranged to meet him in Berlin, so that she could tell him they were going to have a second child. Who in fact was the father? She didn't know. Such things happen, though they rarely give rise to simple situations. While waiting for hers to become very complicated indeed, Alma retired to the Semmering with her two daughters. Franz came to see her when his military duties permitted.

Alma's elder daughter, Gucki, was now an adolescent who hated her nickname and begged to be called by her proper name, Anna. She still had startling blue eyes in a sad little face. She had apparently got used to her mother's succession of lovers, and had got on well with Kokoschka, whom she used to watch as he painted, Gropius, whom she rarely saw, and Werfel, who she knew must not be disturbed when he was working. She was already proficient at the piano, and played duets with Alma. She was a touching little creature, full of memories of her father, overwhelmed by her mother's personality. She was charming with her tiny sister Manon, and helped out as best she could, going for example into the woods to collect the mushrooms which were an important item in the family diet, for as the war went on and on material conditions had become difficult. When she had married again Alma had lost her widow's pension, inflation had whittled away the income she derived from Mahler's works, food was rationed, the farmers in the surrounding countryside kept their products for the local residents they had known before the war, butter was scarce, meat non-existent. But Alma could always cope with practical problems, and her house on the Semmering could still provide a warm welcome to its visitors.

One day Franz Werfel was about to set off from the Hotel Bristol to go and see Alma when he caught sight of Gropius, who had managed to obtain leave to visit his wife. Werfel decided, on reflection, not to accompany him. In July he went out by train to spend the weekend with Alma. She was now seven months pregnant. He was given the room next to Alma's bedroom. 'I didn't control myself. We made love! I didn't spare her. Towards dawn I went back to my room', he wrote later, in his diary.

The maid woke him: her mistress had a haemorrhage, he must go at once to the village to fetch the doctor. He set off at a run, got lost, had to wade through a swamp to get back on to the right road. On the way he made two vows: if God would make everything come right he would remain ever faithful to Alma, and he would give up smoking. He found a doctor at last, and set off back to the house with him. On the way he met Gucki. She at least was keeping her head, and was going down to the village to telephone a doctor in Vienna.

They arrived at the house. Werfel felt miserable, useless. Towards midday Alma summoned him to her room. He went in, and was moved almost to tears by her beauty. In every word she uttered in her low voice there was a wonderful enthusiasm such as only really great people can have when they suffer. Alma is a wonderful person . . . I told her how guilty I felt for what had happened. She said: 'I'm just as guilty as you: not guilty at all. Guilt! For me there is no such thing.'

She looks at things from a sibylline vantage point, in inspired instinct-association leaps. She is one of the few sorceresses of our times. She lives in a luminous magic in which there is a strong desire to destroy, an urge to dominate . . . Alma subjects me again and again to her instinctive insights. She undertook my defence as well as my accusation.

Her perception is sharp and clear. She sees every organ in my body. I believe in her judgements, the good and the bad, especially the bad. I feel myself known by my body and behaviour. She has really acquired great influence over me, because she is there as a power, as a productive organism.

That is a very good portrait of Alma, one with which all of her men could have agreed. Guilt? There was no such thing for her!

Later that day Franz left to return to Vienna. Alma had refused to let the village doctor touch her, 'with his butcher's hands', but Professor Halban was coming from Vienna. And, by fortunate (fortunate?) coincidence, Walter Gropius arrived, having got a lift in an army truck. Professor Halban decided to do a small operation, probably to insert a ring, and then have Alma transported to a hospital in Vienna.

At the Löw Sanatorium, after a long night of suffering, Alma, now 39, gave birth to a premature baby boy. Franz, who had been telephoning all night, finally got through at nine o'clock in the morning. He heard Gropius's voice telling him the news: 'It was a very difficult night. The child is alive. Alma is as well as can be expected. We'll have to wait and see for a few days.' The two men continued to telephone each other frequently for several days. Did Gropius have suspicions? Of what? In any case he behaved as if he had none. He had obtained special leave to stay with his wife.

Werfel came to see her. He was struck by the hospital atmosphere, the small room, white and bare, full of flowers.

It was August, four o'clock in the afternoon, and the heavy air of a summer's day in a big city hung in the room. On the white-painted sickbed lay a woman whom I loved . . . Her long fair hair spread out around her on the pillow. Her face was drained of colour, but never had she looked more gloriously beautiful. The woman I loved was not my wife, not yet. In this dreadful situation I even had to behave like an innocent stranger . . .

Franz Werfel was not a cynical man. He considered himself to be above bourgeois conventions. 'But all the same the icy, searing conviction came over me that we two had sinned not only against bourgeois conventions, but against a higher order of things. Man, woman, child, that sacred coming together ought not to be as it was there and then.'

Before this new-born child of whom he was the father he stood petrified, searching for an emotion which would not come. This pale, silent baby embarrassed him. If only it would cry! But it didn't cry. Franz murmured a few comforting words to Alma. 'Everything will be alright, don't worry', sensed that the nurse was looking at him, and put on an innocent face.

The lie they were living was abruptly shattered. One Sunday morning, early, Alma was talking to Franz on the telephone. They were discussing what name they would give the child. They had already discussed it several times before, and now agreed on Martin. Suddenly Gropius came into the room, a bunch of flowerrs in his hand. He heard Alma using the intimate 'Du' form to Franz Werfel, and the tone in which she was speaking to him left no room for doubt. She saw her husband, and hung up. Gropius calmly said: 'He's your lover, isn't he?' She made no reply. Now he knew.

That afternoon he went to see Werfel. But Werfel was taking a nap and didn't hear him knocking. So he left his card, with a note scribbled on it: 'I have come to beseech you, with all the strength I can summon up. For the love of God, be careful with Alma. A disaster could happen. The excitement . . . suppose we [we!] lost the child!' He then left to rejoin his unit. 'When I read this extremely noble message I didn't know where to put myself. I thought I would faint', wrote Werfel, not feeling very proud of himself.

Some days later, now back at home with her baby (in those days doctors had little idea of how to treat premature babies) Alma received a letter from her husband. He was prepared to let her have a divorce if he could have custody of Manon. She replied refusing the offer: she would never give up Manon.

Was there now going to be the usual painful haggle between estranged parents over the custody of their child? Not quite. Walter Gropius was not a simple man. One evening in November 1918 Alma saw him coming up to the house. Franz was with him. Gropius had fetched him from his hotel. Lieutenant Gropius was no longer in the army. The tragedy of the collapse of Germany had begun. But it was his own personal tragedy that he now wanted to settle.

'Go away' shouted Alma, 'go away, both of you. I will have nothing further to do with you, Walter, nor with you, Franz. And you shan't lay a finger on the children, they are mine!' Then followed an incredible spectacle. Walter Gropius threw himself at his wife's feet, beat his breast, implored her to forgive him . . . It was all his fault! All he wanted was to keep her, nothing else. Would she consent to remain his wife?

At this Alma, before whom it was always a mistake to humble oneself, lost what remained of her love for Gropius. Franz Werfel, an embarrassed spectator but also directly involved, watched this scene with mixed feelings and tried to calm things down. He succeeded eventually, but in the days which followed it was he who lost his calm. He peremptorily summoned Alma to have done with Gropius once and for all. She was only temporizing with him because of Manon.

Alma wrote later: 'During this time, the monarchy was collapsing, but I was more concerned with my own problems. I scarcely noticed that event of world importance.' On the other hand, she could not ignore the events that shook Vienna on 11 November 1918. She had to take notice this time, if only because Franz Werfel was actively involved.

Everything began, as always, with an angry crowd gathering in the streets to march on the Parliament. From the window of her red drawing-room Alma watched the 'procession of proletarians' passing by, heard the sounds of shooting, took from a drawer the revolver she was now never without. That day Emperor Karl I had announced that he would take no further part in affairs of state, and formally relieved the prime minister of the last imperial government of his duties. The Austrian Republic was proclaimed. The red, white, and red flag was about to be hoisted when the crowd launched its assault on the Parliament buildings. In the ensuing tumult the communists tore the white stripe out of the flag and hoisted what remained as a red flag. Rioters broke the windows of the Café Landtmann, a habitual meeting-place of the prosperous bourgeoisie. The customers fled in panic. The disorder continued throughout the night.

The next day Franz Werfel, in uniform, came to ask Alma's blessing before going off to join in the revolution. 'In my heart I was against it' wrote Alma later. She thought the whole thing was senseless, but kissed him on the brow all the same. He came back in the evening, dirty, clothes torn, 'smelling of cheap liquor and tobacco', and told her that the young intellectuals had founded the Red Guard. Furious, she sent him away again.

He had spent the whole day standing on the park benches of the Ring, exhorting the rioters to 'take the banks by storm', and shouting 'down with the capitalists'. But the revolution took a different course, and the result was a bourgeois republic, reduced to the boundaries it possesses today, and the end of the Habsburg dynasty.

When order had been restored on the streets, respectable bourgeois opinion in Vienna condemned Franz Werfel for the part he had played. Berta Zuckerkandl was the only one to defend him. He was wanted by the police. Who would save him? Walter Gropius, whose relations with the husbands and lovers of his wife were curious indeed, with his splendid war record (wounded four times, twice awarded the Iron Cross), he came forward as guarantor for Franz Werfel. After which he went back to Berlin to look for work to support his family, leaving Alma to Franz. She was now no longer sure that she still wanted Werfel, although she was still enjoying 'glorious nights' with him.

She let him stay in her house on the Semmering, while she remained in Vienna. Within a week he had written the first act of a play, *Der Spiegelmensch* (The Mirror Man), in which he settled accounts with his former friend, Karl Kraus. Then, tired of being alone, he returned to Vienna, where Alma made a scene on hearing that he had decided to spend Christmas with his relatives in Prague. She failed to make him change his mind, and off he went, leaving her alone with her children: starry-eyed Gucki, now called Anna, already taller than her mother; Manon, at two-and-a-half years of age already showing some of Alma's charms; and little Martin, frail, so frail.

Alma had engaged an English nurse to look after the baby, but now had to manage the house with the help of only one maid, Ida. Fortunately, Anna Moll was there, as diligent and efficient as ever. Alma was good at getting things done, but not at doing things herself.

Food and coal were desperately scarce. Berta Zuckerkandl set about persuading her old friend Clemenceau to agree to the setting up of an inter-allied food commission, which he had so far opposed with his veto. She wrote to him: 'Georges, I know that you are intent on destroying Austria as a punishment for what she has done . . . Vienna, the city whose carefree charm you loved, is today the scene of a frightful tragedy. No, you mustn't do a thing like that'. Whether for the sake of memories of his youth, or for considerations of political expediency, the 'Tiger' gave way. And Berta was able to write in her memoirs: 'My friendship with Clemenceau was thus to bear splendid fruit.' The threat of starvation receded.

In January little Martin had to be taken to hospital to undergo an operation, a cranial puncture. For the first time Alma experienced a certain sense of unworthiness. This sweet innocent child was having to suffer, and it was her fault. Yet she didn't even know for certain who his father was! She was ashamed. While Martin lay dying in hospital, she cast her mind back over her life. She told herself she had never made a mistake, there was nothing she needed to recant, but she wondered nevertheless 'how I ever found peace and quiet in the minds of those men'. What should she now do? Should she get a divorce from Gropius? The vestige of bourgeois conventionality she still retained held her back. Suppose he were, after all, the best of the husbands she could have? She had promised she would take his daughter to him. At the beginning of March she joined him in Berlin. But there he talked of taking them with him to live in Weimar, where he had just set up the Bauhaus. And she thought: 'What! Vegetate in Weimar with Walter Gropius for the rest of my days?'

A telegram came, addressed to Gropius, legally the father of Martin. The child had died. 'If only I could have died instead of him', said Gropius, breaking the news to Alma. Then impeccable as ever, he sent a telegram to Werfel.

Alma was now thoroughly confused. She no longer wanted Gropius, she no longer wanted Werfel, 'the source of all my misfortune'. She wanted Kokoschka, who had just let her know, using Baron Dirzstay as his messenger, that without her he simply could not paint any more. Making the excuse that she felt she ought to leave Gropius alone for a while with his daughter, she went into Berlin to look for Kokoschka.

As luck would have it she didn't find him. If she had the situation would have become even more complicated. She returned from her expedition crestfallen and sad, but having finally made up her mind to go through with the divorce. Walter Gropius was then much preoccupied with interesting developments in his professional life, which may have made him more open to the idea of finally losing Alma. But as far as Manon was concerned, he wouldn't budge. He insisted on having custody.

Alma went back to Vienna and found Franz more infatuated than ever, young, eager, loving, generous, spendthrift, his head full of plans . . . To welcome her home he had prepared a table loaded with sumptuous dishes—they were both passionately fond of eating. And he said the right things in his letters to her: 'Almitschka, live for me! I see my future only in you. I want to marry you. Not only because I love you, but because I know in my heart that if there is one person on earth who can bring me fulfilment and make an artist of me, you are that person.'

With that splendid assurance which never failed her, that faith in her own light, she took charge of him, began to rule him with an iron hand. Henceforth he would have to work to earn the right to see her. 'Franz is a tiny bird in my hand,' she wrote, 'with beating heart and watchful eyes, whom I must protect from the weather and the cats. Sometimes he tries to be a hero, but I like him better as a little bird, because the other side of him doesn't need me, nor anyone else probably.'

But she didn't want to marry for a third time. Why should she? Society had changed. She was now 40 years old. She could live as she wished without official sanction from the registry office. She wanted to travel, she detested the 'politicization' of Vienna, which had recovered in the meanwhile a large part of its luxury life-style and particular charm.

'Yes, and now politics!' she wrote,

I would like to see the emperor come back—even if he turned out to be the biggest idiot of them all—and the most expensive archdukes with large families, whom the country would have to support. Let's have splendour and pomp to look up to again, and a knuckling under, a silent knuckling under, of the servile lower orders . . .

The howling of the masses is a hellish music which a refined ear can never bear to hear. Tolstoy thought he heard angels in it, but it was his own voice he was hearing, just as in great silences or empty spaces the sound of your own blood pulsing rushes in from outside.

Another trip to Weimar did little to make her like 'the masses' better. After the feverish interlude of the communist republic in Bavaria, a general strike was declared throughout Germany. There was no water, no electricity. Alma and Manon left their hotel and took refuge in Gropius's apartment, though the builders and decorators were still working on it.

The stink of corpses hung in the streets. On the day the workers killed during the demonstrations were buried, Alma watched from the window a passing procession carrying placards with the inscriptions: 'Long live Rosa Luxemburg!', 'Long live Liebknecht!' The Architects' Association was present in the ranks almost to a man. Gropius regretted that he had followed Alma's advice, and was not with them. He told her so. 'I just wanted him to keep out of politics', she wrote.

Like many people, Alma believed that the best way to avoid trouble was 'to keep out of politics'. She left Weimar in haste, taking her daughter with her. But this time Gropius had agreed that they would divorce, and that Alma should have custody of Manon, but only on condition that he could see her regularly. He wrote Alma a letter to that effect on 12 July 1919.

Some time later Alma went to Holland with her other daughter, Anna, to be present at the Mahler festival organized by Willem Mengelberg. She found it boring, oh so boring, even though she was treated like royalty. The speeches, the thanks, being presented to the royal family, giving her blessing to the foundation of a Mahler society—she loathed every minute of it. Mahler's widow? But he had died ten years ago! And she had a living genius to look after now. At least she considered him as such. He was muddle-headed, emotional, unstable, vacillating between the Christian and the Jewish faiths which he claimed to be reconciling in his works, vacillating between Marxism and the conservatism he would end up by advocating, vacillating as to his identity, a man from nowhere not knowing where

his homeland was (Prague? Vienna?) now that the Empire had
disintegrated. But he was working hard, and his career was developing.
His adaptation of *The Trojan Women* was now playing at the Burgtheater in Vienna. His play *Bockgesang* was being put on in Leipzig,
the *Spiegelmensch* was being performed in Prague and Munich. A
little book of his entitled *The Victim, not the Murderer, is the Guilty One*
(an idea he owed to Alma), created quite a stir.

None of this brought in much money, but his father paid him a
monthly allowance, and kept asking when Franz would introduce
him to the woman he had said he was going to marry. Alma was in no
hurry. The difference in their ages worried her, especially now that
her daughter Anna had got engaged, at 17, to Rupert Koller, the son
of a family they were friends with. Alma was not exactly thrilled at the
idea that she might shortly be a grandmother. Nevertheless, she gave
them her blessing. Grandmother? Two impassioned declarations of
love, one from the orchestral conductor Ochs, the other from the
poet Trentini, arrived just in time to soften the impact of the
prospect: grandmother perhaps, but still irresistible. Her spirits were
also raised thanks to Maurice Ravel, whom the indefatigable Berta
had brought to Vienna for a series of concerts of his music.

It was arranged that he would stay at Alma's. She found Ravel's
'mask of perversity' amusing, while appreciating his culture and
refined sensitivity. In the morning, at breakfast, he would appear,
complete with make-up and perfume, in a brilliant taffeta dressing-
gown . . . He took evident delight in playing the part.

He was enchanted with Vienna. One day he went into a leather
shop and bought two bags. He gave his name to the manageress: she
refused to let him pay. 'What do you think of that?' he said to Berta, 'I
could live in Paris a hundred years, and that would never happen!'
The concerts were a great success. Alma and Berta organized a
farewell party for Ravel, Viennese style, with plenty of *Heuriger*, the
local wine straight from the harvest. All the Viennese artists were
there. Ravel kept asking the musicians to play Strauss waltzes, kissed
everyone within reach, and loved it.

On his return to France he composed his famous waltz-poem *La
Valse*, in which the rhythm at the end changes into a *danse macabre*. 'I
conceived that work', he said later, 'as a kind of apotheosis of the
Viennese waltz which turns in my mind into a merry-go-round with

death.' He had sensed the chaos that threatened behind the festive façade.

One day, on an impulse, Alma bought a house in Venice. She was not predicting the future, perhaps, but a confused foreboding played a part in her decision. Venice, she thought, was a possible refuge. It was there that she met Kokoschka in the street, and he asked her to meet him in the Café Florian, and then failed to turn up.

She would have searched the town for him, but Franz arrived. They were living together in Vienna, but Alma insisted on periods of separation during which Franz had to work if he wanted to see her again. The discipline was effective. He worked, 'produced', was moderately successful. Real success would only come in the early 1930s. For the time being he was working hard, sometimes on the Semmering, sometimes in Italy, on a biography of Verdi.

In 1924 he was in Prague when he received a call from his friend Max Brod. Max had just arrived from Berlin with Franz Kafka, who was dying. They arranged for Kafka to be taken to the Wiener Wald Sanatorium, and then to Professor Hayek's clinic, where he was put into the general ward. Brod argued that he should have a room of his own. Franz came up and expostulated with Professor Hayek. The Professor replied: 'Someone called Werfel is asking me to do something for someone called Kafka. Kafka I know, he's Bed Number 12. But who is Werfel?' Werfel never told Alma that story.

That same year they travelled to Egypt and Palestine and she also accompanied him on his lecture tours. They were together in Berlin for the première of *Wozzek*, the opera which Alban Berg had dedicated to Alma. The success of the première made Berg known internationally. They then went on to Prague, again to a performance of *Wozzek*. Prague was no longer Austrian, it was now the capital of Czechoslovakia. Alma was furious when she was held up at the frontier because she did not have a return visa, but a solution was eventually found. This time the opera was not well received. The Bürgermeister of Prague had attended the dress rehearsal, during which he had a stroke which proved fatal. Press reports alleged that he had been outraged by Berg's music. The première took place on the day of his funeral. Some Prague citizens were therefore predisposed to be hostile.

As soon as the curtain went up protests broke out. The box in

which the Bergs, Alma, and Franz were sitting was quickly identified
by the flowers with which it was decorated. Insults were shouted.
The conductor took to his heels. Further shouts came from the
audience: 'Shame on you! Jew! Jew!', meaning the Bergs. They left
the theatre under police protection. Berg was not Jewish, nor was his
wife—she was the illegitimate daughter of Emperor Franz Josef!

'Politics' caught up with Alma again in July 1927, in Vienna. The
workers set fire to the Law Courts. The mounted police opened fire.
Ninety people were killed. Chancellor Seipel, whom the socialists
nicknamed 'the prelate without pity', defended the brutality of his
repressive measures against criticism from the social democrats.
Alma's comments in her diary refer, as one would expect, to 'mobs
running wild'. But she continued:

Intellectuals can be scholars, artists, financiers, but they should keep their
hands off politics. They set the world on fire with their lack of imagination.
People should put a stop to their machinations before it's too late.

Intellect in politics is the greatest misfortune in Europe and Asia.

Civilizations are trampled underfoot and destroyed, and 'in the name of
humanity' human beings are being massacred.

Austria is already lost. It might perhaps be saved by the Caesarean
operation: union with Germany. But then it will wake up and no
longer understand its own blood. For Austria will then be the vassal of
Germany . . .

She wasn't far from the mark.

The repressive government measures provoked a general strike
throughout the country. Alma had just had electricity installed on the
Semmering. Now she had none. She concluded: 'It's nonsense to
think that the machine is an outward means of helping us on the way
to inner freedom. The more we depend on it, the more surely the
worker will become our tsar. When we still worked with candles, it
was not so easy for things from outside to happen to us.'

And yet Vienna still retained that indefinable something that had
always enchanted its guests. The following year, when Berta Zuckerkandl finally managed to perusade her old friend Paul Painlevé, the
French Minister for War, to come to Austria under the aegis of the
Alliance pour la Culture, and gave a reception for him to which of
course Alma and Franz were invited, Painlevé said:

In spite of all that has happened, this city still has a strange charm that gives it a fairy-tale quality. People are so different here. These Viennese men and women have something of the naïve unconcern of children: yes, that is a significant feature of the way this city conducts its life. I have travelled a lot, I know something of the élites in many countries, but nowhere else have I found this simplicity, this calm smile. It is the smile of a people impregnated with a very ancient culture.

Vienna was not going to smile much longer.

10. Frau Alma Werfel

In 1929, Alma had two worries: her daughter Anna who, following in her mother's footsteps, was divorcing for the second time (after Koller she had married a young composer, Ernst Krenek), and her age. She had been able to verify from time to time that her seductive power had not diminished. Gerhart Hauptmann, with whom she had recently spent an evening or two, needed no more than a few drinks to call her his 'great love', and to tell her that 'in another life we must be lovers'. At which his wife had chipped in: 'There too you'll have to wait your turn.' Kokoschka had written to her urging her to come away with him to Africa.

When she looked at herself in the mirror, she saw a face that was almost without blemish, framed now in bobbed hair. The intense blue of her eyes, the head carried high, the perfect outline of her lips, the delicate nose—all that was unchanged. Her body, however, had filled out due to too much rich food, too much alcohol. But she dressed it well, as always. Now that women were showing their legs, she readily showed hers, which were long, shapely, and always clad in the finest silk stockings. Her waist, in the old days squeezed into a corset, had never been slim. It had not improved, but with the modern fashion such things could be camouflaged. And to the end of her life she boasted that she never wore a girdle. At 50, Alma was still superb.

But she was tired. On some footling pretext, she had a violent row with Franz. She had had enough of the 'enslavement of women through male domination'. As they get older women have a tendency to kick over the traces. Alma had long ago finished with the delights of submissiveness, always assuming that she had ever enjoyed them for any length of time. Keeping house for Franz Werfel, fetching and carrying for him, really, was that a job that could absorb the energy, intelligence, and talent of a woman like Alma? Was this the blind alley to which her youthful ambitions had led? She did not always have such thoughts, but when the mood came over her, she felt she was suffocating. Then, what better way of filling her lungs with air than by staging a scene with the man she had under her thumb?

She left for Venice with Anna. She found Venice boring, and went on to Rome, to visit Mussolini's mistress, Margherita Sarfatti. The two women had a serious conversation. After having observed that only a world organization could change the course of events, La Sarfatti went on to explain that 'an international fascism would only be possible if fascism in other countries took a leaf out of Mussolini's book and avoided the Jewish question'. Alma was reassured. 'I had only gone to see her to discuss that question', she wrote. She did not know that Margherita Sarfatti was herself Jewish. And that one day Mussolini would change mistresses.

A conversation with the insufferable Pfitzner, who happened to be passing through Vienna, took a nasty turn. Alma had brought out a few bottles of Tokay, to which she helped herself generously, as did Pfitzner and Franz. The two men fell out on the subject of Hitler, and Pfitzner, raising his fist, shouted: 'Hitler will soon show you! Germany will win in spite of everything!'

Tragic news came to them: Arthur Schnitzler's only daughter had committed suicide in Venice. She had shot herself with a revolver. She had been married to an Italian colonel. Alma described in her diary how she visited Schnitzler, and found him prostrate with grief. She added: 'Last night I decided not to get married. The reason for this new estrangement is a poem Franz Werfel is now writing, a poem on the death of Lenin!'

Later she wrote: 'For ten years I have been uncertain of myself, playing some sort of role, outwardly the happy beloved of a well-known poet. But I don't feel I'm either his beloved or his wife. And he wants us to get married, as quickly as possible, but something in me says no.' And then a few days later: 'Perhaps I'll marry Franz Werfel after all. He is the kindest, most affectionate man in my life.'

And finally: 'I couldn't live without Jews, indeed I live all the time almost only with them. But I often hate them so much that I could scream.' It is perhaps hardly necessary to point out that her use of the plural in this context never failed to drive Werfel berserk.

To cut a long story short, on 8 July 1929 Alma Schindler-Mahler-Gropius married Franz Werfel. The perplexity of little Manon, who could not quite understand what role Franz was playing in her mother's life, may have persuaded Alma finally to make up her mind. The day before the wedding, she wrote:

I am not well physically.

Breaking down on all fronts. My eyes no longer work. My hands move more slowly at the piano. Eating, standing, walking—it's all too much for me. The most I can do is drink. And that is often the only way of overcoming the chills and shivers I feel in my body, for I am a vagotonic and have a slow pulse and a weak heart.

In a few weeks I shall be 50 years of age—and Franz Werfel is young. I must keep up with him, act young. Must devote my whole interest in life to his career—not, as I would like, stand objectively above things.

Shortly thereafter her daughter Anna got married for the third time, to Paul von Zsolnay, a member of the well-to-do family who were Franz's publishers. Alma greeted the news without enthusiasm. This time, she was sure, she was going to be a grandmother. Indeed, Anna did then have a child, before divorcing for a third time, after which she embarked on a career as a sculptress, not without success, and further marital adventures. Surrounded by the reflected glory of her father's name, crushed beneath a dominating mother who fascinated her, haunted from childhood by her sister's death, it is understandable that she should have found it difficult to stand on her own two feet. Besides, who would have wanted to be Alma's daughter?

More tragic news: Hugo von Hofmannsthal had died. His eldest son, Franz, had committed suicide at the age of 26. On the day of the funeral, just as he was taking his place at the head of the cortege of mourners, Hugo von Hofmannsthal had collapsed and died. He was 55. Cherished idol of the Viennese intelligentsia, he had long wanted to die. He had written these prophetic words: 'Politics is magic. People are going to follow the man who can conjure up the dark forces from the depths.' They wouldn't have to wait much longer. But in 1929, in Vienna, it was still possible to delude oneself. The Devil's writ still did not extend to Austria.

Franz and Alma set off on their honeymoon, revisiting Egypt and Palestine, and going on to the Lebanon. There the sight of so much misery and squalor disgusted Alma, but Franz, impressed by the sufferings of the Armenian refugees, felt his writer's imagination stir. He talked things over with Alma and together they worked out a scenario. The result was *The Forty Days of Musa Dagh*, a moving historical novel. It became Franz Werfel's first outstanding success, made him internationally known, and earned him consideration for a Nobel prize. On their return, the Werfels held a house-warming party in the twenty-eight-room house Alma had just purchased on the Hohe Warte. All Vienna was present.

Franz was now the most well-known of Austrian authors: he had been awarded the Schiller prize, and was the quasi-official poet laureate. Alma was the capital city's leading hostess. Klaus Mann wrote the following description of her at that time:

Frau Alma, who had close links with Schuschnigg [Federal Chancellor and leader of the Clerical Party] and his followers, held her salon, the meeting-place for *tout Vienne*: government, church, diplomacy, literature, music, theatre—they were all there. The mistress of the house, tall, impeccably turned out, still imposing in face and figure, moved triumphantly from the Papal Nuncio to Richard Strauss or Arnold Schönberg, from the Minister to the *Heldentenor*, from the elegantly gaga old aristocrat to the promising young poet. In a corner of the boudoir people were negotiating in whispers over the allocation of a high government post, while in another group the cast for a new comedy at the Burgtheater was being decided.

In the sumptuous house in which she received her guests, Alma exhibited, like a huntswoman, her trophies which every visitor had respectfully to admire. In a glass case was the manuscript of the Tenth Symphony, the one which contained the composer's last cries of love. It was open at the appropriate page, for all to see. On the wall hung a portrait of Alma as Lucrezia Borgia, by Kokoschka. There were also the live trophies: Franz Werfel, whom Musil had nicknamed 'the fire hydrant' in tribute to his gushing eloquence. And the exquisite 16-year-old Manon.

Elias Canetti, who hated Alma but nevertheless frequented her salon in the early 1930s because he was in love with Anna Mahler, wrote a cruel portrait of her after their first encounter: 'A rather tall woman, overflowing in all directions, with a sugary smile and shining, staring eyes . . . The legend of her beauty had continued to make the rounds for thirty years, and now there she was, lowering herself heavily into a chair, slightly tipsy'.

Alma first took him round the items in her private museum, and then called Manon: 'After a moment a gazelle came tripping lightly into the room, a delicate, brown creature, dressed as a young girl, untouched by the luxurious surroundings into which it had been summoned . . . it radiated shyness even more than beauty—an angel's gazelle, not from the Ark, but from heaven.' Canetti wanted to wrest her from this 'den of depravity', but Alma was saying:

She's lovely, isn't she? Well, that's Manon, my daughter. From Gropius. Nobody can hold a candle to her. You don't mind my saying that, do you Annie? Why shouldn't you have a beautiful sister! Like father, like daughter. Have you ever seen Gropius? A tall, handsome fellow. Aryan to his finger-tips. The only man who matches me racially. The others who fell in love with me were all little Jews, like Mahler.

Canetti left, horrified, but that didn't prevent him from coming back again whenever he was invited.

This society life was interesting and amusing, but it was not enough to take Alma out of herself. So, old Nietzschean though she was, she turned to religion for help, in addition to the Benedictine she now imbibed from morning to night. She began by placating her conscience in a general confession at the Cathedral of St Stephen. Then she found the man she needed. She met him at the enthrone-ment of Cardinal Innitzer. A lunch followed the ceremony, and Alma was introduced to a handsome priest, 38 years of age, Johannes Hollnsteiner, a professor of theology who it was said would himself one day put on the cardinal's purple.

The intimate relationship which then developed between them (to call it 'friendship' would be to understate its closeness) naturally exasperated Franz Werfel, although he could see the ridiculous side of being jealous of a man of the cloth. Mornings and afternoons, Hollnsteiner and Alma were always together.

Men had composed for her, painted for her, but no one before had said mass for her. It raised her to the clouds. She floated in an ecstasy of adoration; she confided in her diary that she wanted to kneel before him, submit to him; she exulted when he told her: 'I have never been close to any woman. You are the first and you will be the last.' How close? She noted one day in her diary: 'Hollnsteiner is either an angel or a scoundrel. Out of respect for myself I have decided to think of him as an angel . . . The following words have been crossed out. So we shall never know exactly what the scoundrel did.

What we do know is that he had a soft spot for Hitler, and profoundly influenced Alma. One evening in 1933 the Werfels invited H. G. Wells, Dorothy Thompson, and Sinclair Lewis to their home. They had just been expelled from Germany, and told of what they had seen. All the same, said Alma and Franz, there is some good in what Hitler is doing . . . And Alma wrote: 'When I look at Hitler, who spent fourteen years in the wilderness because his time was not yet come, I see in him a genuine German idealist, something which is unthinkable for the Jews.' Some years later she crossed out that sentence, and added: 'Unfortunately, he is stupid.' Stupid was perhaps not quite the right word.

On Hollnsteiner's advice she made no protest when the German authorities ordered Werfel's works to be burnt, and banned Mahler's music. She was blinded by what were then called the achievements of fascism, and she wasn't the only one. Franz Werfel was at first quite convinced that he would be accepted into the Nazi Association of German Writers. He signed a declaration of loyalty to the Hitler regime. He described himself in his application as a member of the German community of Czechoslovakia. Incredible? Yes, but he did it all the same. He was not a great man. There are very few great men. He was a great writer. He wanted so much to go on being read in Germany, and touring the German cities giving his well-known public readings from his own works and the German classics. However, the Association of German Writers turned him down, his public readings were banned, and he began after all to have some doubts.

In Berlin in April 1933 200 policemen invaded the Bauhaus, then located in a former factory. Thirty students were arrested. The Bauhaus was denounced as a 'source of degenerate art', and a 'breeding-place for Bolshevist culture'. Gropius was no longer its director, and the authorities left him alone. Like many architects he was naïve enough to believe that he could persuade people that architecture had nothing to do with politics, that it was a pure expression of modern thought and therefore compatible with any regime. He became a member of the Reich Chamber for the Plastic Arts, took part in a competition sponsored by the Nazi 'German Labour Front' organization, and mounted an exhibition entitled 'The German People' for it. He was on the slippery slope that led to active involvement in the regime. But Gropius was not a Nazi. He dropped everything and emigrated to London. And later he made a second, brilliant career for himself in the United States.

Refugees from Germany began to arrive in Austria. 'The rats are boarding the sinking ship', Karl Kraus sneered. The situation inside the country got worse from day to day. The little, almost dwarfish, Chancellor Dollfuss, popularly known as 'Millimetternich', shut down the Parliament and governed by emergency decrees.

Under pressure from Mussolini and the Austrian Heimwehr (paramilitary homeguard), he took the crazy decision to destroy Austrian social democracy once and for all. In the capital and some other industrial towns the Heimwehr and the armed forces stormed the social democrat strongpoints. In Vienna the government ordered troops to occupy the Town Hall, the socialists tried to retake it. There was heavy fighting in the streets.

Charles Rist, an envoy from the French Foreign Ministry, telephoned to Berta Zuckerkandl, who was expecting him for lunch: 'I am in the French Embassy. I can't come. Can't you hear the machine-guns? Austria is committing suicide.' The fighting lasted three days. The social democrats were crushed. All that was left was to get rid of Dollfuss. In July 1934 the Chancellor, Engelbert Dollfuss, was assassinated by the Austrian Nazis.

The news made little impression on the Werfels. They were overwhelmed by a tragic turn in their family affairs. One evening in April they had arrived in Venice to join Manon. They had found her pale, complaining of frightful headaches. Alma had at once called a doctor, and asked her mother to come to them. Within a few hours the girl's whole body was stricken with paralysis: poliomyelitis. She was 17 years old.

At first the doctors were confident. As soon as he heard that his beloved daughter was ill, Gropius came from London to spend a week with her. They promised him she would recover the use of her legs. Alma was convinced of it. Manon's condition would improve, because she, Alma, wanted it to! There was, in fact, very little improvement. But now Manon, delightful Manon, dressed, adorned, moved in a wheelchair around the spacious house on the Hohe Warte.

There followed a grim comedy. Under the influence of Father Hollnsteiner Alma had the diabolical idea of getting Manon engaged, to a young man recommended by the good father. 'She will get well', said Alma. 'Being happy at the side of her fiancé will make her well.' Poor little Manon. One day she could stand it no longer. 'Let me die in peace,' she begged. 'I shall never get well.' Then she said: 'You'll get over it, Mummy, as you get over everything, as everybody gets over everything.' And she died, quite suddenly, on Easter Monday 1935.

In memory of Manon Gropius, Alban Berg wrote his violin concerto *Dem Andenken eines Engels* (To the memory of an angel). The funeral ceremony took place in the cemetery at Grinzing. Everything was done very quickly because of the risk of contagion. Informed too late, Walter Gropius could not get there in time. Manon was not buried in Mahler's grave, but in another vault a hundred yards away. Here is a description of the ceremony as seen by the unforgiving Canetti:

On this occasion, too, everything was done for effect. All Vienna was there. That is to say, all those who were usually invited to the parties at the Hohe Warte. Others who would have loved to receive such invitations but never managed it were also there. It's impossible to prevent people from coming to a funeral . . .

We were standing not far from the open grave, and I heard the moving words spoken by Hollnsteiner, to whom the mourning mother's heart belonged. She was weeping, and it struck me that even her tears were unusually large. There were not too many, but she managed to weep so that they flowed together larger than life-size. Tears such as I had never seen, like enormous pearls, a precious adornment. One couldn't see them without marvelling at so much motherly love.

Of course the young girl had borne her suffering, as Hollnsteiner so eloquently said, with superhuman patience, but oh how great had been the suffering of the mother who had had to stand and watch it all for a whole long year . . .

Whether or not Alma had exploited to the full her role of afflicted mother before the crowd of her acquaintances, she was certainly genuinely and deeply moved, perhaps for the first time, though this was the third child she had lost. She knew, this time, that she would have no more. She did not give way, but she had aged. Her fair hair was now white. She hid her arms under long sleeves, her waist under jackets, she dressed in black. She sold her house in Venice, full as it was of Manon's presence.

Franz Werfel was very near to her, ever ready to help her through this ordeal. But he was now the star. It was about him that the newspapers wrote; it was he who was invited to New York, though she went along with him, for the performance of his dramatic oratorio *Der Weg der Verheissung* (The Eternal Road); it was for him, the author of *The Forty Days of Musa Dagh*, that the Armenian community of New York gave a gala evening to express its gratitude; it was he who was invited to a debate on the future of literature organized in Paris by the League of Nations; and it was he who spent all his evenings in cafés with James Joyce—the two of them finally getting thrown out because they sang Verdi's arias together, at the top of their voices.

And Alma wrote: 'My marriage is a marriage no longer. I live unhappily alongside Werfel, whose monologues are now never-ending. It's always his intentions, his words, his, his, his! He has forgotten how important my words once were for him.' Now, as before, the only world she was prepared to acknowledge was one of which she was the centre.

But now that world was falling apart. They were travelling in Italy, in 1938, when the news reached them: the Chancellor Schuschnigg was with Hitler in Berchtesgaden. At any moment now Austria was going to be annexed by Germany. Mere chance had spared Franz Werfel from being in Vienna, where he could have been beaten to death by the young Austrian Nazis. He would never see his country again. And Alma, 'the impeccable Christian'? What was she going to do? Abandon him? Leave this Jew who had now become more dangerous than a loaded revolver? Go back to Austria and 'keep out of politics'?

She left Franz behind in Italy and took the train to Vienna. She had warned no one of her return, except Ida, her maid. She took a room in a hotel, and then went out into the town, her Vienna, which she could no longer recognize. In the street she met by chance the wife of the Minister of Education, who seemed scared out of her wits. Further on, before the glass front of the offices of the German services, from which a portrait of Hitler proudly looked out, piles of flowers had been heaped. She telephoned her daughter Anna, and found her unconcerned. Yet she was no longer a young girl, she was 37. But she did not seem to understand the danger that threatened a daughter of Mahler. Apropos, one of the first things the Nazis did was to give the Mahlerstrasse another name.

Alma contacted Father Hollnsteiner, who read her a sermon on the greatness of fascism on the march. Finally she went to the Molls. She found them jubilant—not Anna Moll perhaps, she wasn't so sure, she was worried for Alma—but Carl, his daughter Maria, and son-in-law Eberstaller were all resolutely in favour of the Nazis. Alma met a few anti-Nazi friends who talked a lot about the referendum on annexation announced by Chancellor Schuschnigg. They were utterly convinced that the tide was now going to turn. Anna was one of these optimists, and was working with them.

Alma, sceptical in spite of Hollnsteiner's arguments, went to the bank, withdrew her liquid assets, and sewed them in a belt for Ida, who had volunteered to take the money to Switzerland. She packed a few bags, stuffed Mahler's manuscripts into a valise. She then went to the Molls to say goodbye to her mother, entrusted all she possessed in the way of works of art to Carl Moll and appointed him her trustee.

On 11 March the referendum was cancelled. Hitler would be entering the city on 14 March. Hollnsteiner, constantly at Alma's side during these days, still didn't seem to understand what was going on. 'He hadn't the slightest idea', wrote Alma. This man without the slightest idea was to spend eleven months in Dachau, leave the church, and get married. In 1954, by then professor at Linz University, he wrote to Alma: 'Thanks to you, and what you did for me, I became another man.' All things considered, he was the most original, though not the most brilliant, of Alma's conquests.

In spite of the cancellation of the referendum, Anna still didn't want to think of leaving Vienna. Alma had to exert all her maternal authority to persuade her to leave, with her, the next day. Alma spent her last night in Vienna in her hotel room in the company of Hollnsteiner, who was heartbroken at the prospect of her departure. Aircraft were criss-crossing the sky above the capital to announce the arrival of Hitler on the following Monday. On the Ring, where Schuschnigg's supporters had continued demonstrating until the cancellation of the referendum, the Nazis were now going around in their thousands hoisting swastika flags everywhere. As they forced their way into one building after another, some of the inhabitants threw themselves from the windows. Austria had ceased to exist.

The puffed-up, powerful Third Reich gobbled up with relish its rickety, tired little neighbour. Hitler returned in triumph to the land he had once left as a ragged down-and-out. Was it not inevitable? The mass arrests, suicides, executions, the orgy of the pogroms, the shrill din of the propaganda lies, the shrieks of the tortured, and the shouts of joy (yes, a sadistic, ragtaggle mob, drunk with Goebbels' twaddle and the smell of blood, exulted with wanton stupidity), even the lame reaction of the 'world', the cowardly lethargy of the Western democracies: all the elements were there . . . (Klaus Mann)

11. Refugees

In trains which they had to fight to get into, going via Prague, Budapest, Zagreb, and Trieste, Alma and her daughter finally managed to reach Milan, where they found Franz half-dead with worry. From now on they were emigrants, with no fixed abode. They were safe at least, or so they thought. They went to Zurich, to Franz's sister. There Ida Gebauer, reliable as ever, was waiting for them, and handed over the tidy sum of money which she had smuggled through in her belt. But they decided to move on, obtained visas for France, went to Paris, and found rooms in a modest hotel, the Royal-Madeleine. Alma went on, alone, to London, and the others followed later.

But London got Alma down. Her daughter Anna's English was as good as her German. Franz, gifted for languages, quickly brushed up his knowledge. But Alma, in spite of her frequent sojourns in the United States, stubbornly refused to make the effort. It was up to the others to speak her language. The trouble was that they couldn't. She was experiencing the profound distress of those who have lost their home, their friends, their books, their familiar surroundings, and are too old to adjust easily to a new way of life.

Very soon, she began to loathe London. Not only was it 'a cold, clammy city in which the sheets were always damp', but the people were 'a wretched lot' who couldn't have cared less what had happened to Austria. The fatal indifference of the democracies! Could it be that she had been mistaken in the past, and that one should after all take an interest in politics?

For Franz, things were not so difficult. He was in touch with his publishers, dinners were given in his honour, he discovered a taste for whisky. But he dreamt of having a little house somewhere in which he could write. There would be books, a piano . . .

Alma went to look for one, but in France. She settled Franz in the Pavillon Henri IV, in Saint-Germain, so that he could work there, and went prospecting in the south, where many anti-Hitler German intellectuals had already settled. At Sanary-sur-Mer, in the Var, she finally discovered an old watch-tower that had been tastefully converted. They stayed there for some months, while Franz worked on a novel about the fall of Vienna: *Cella oder die Überwinder*. It was there that Alma learnt by telephone of the death of her mother and by radio of the abdication of the great powers in the face of Hitler at Munich. But the French did not seem to be any better than the English at understanding what was happening in the heart of Europe. 'The French!' she wrote, 'outwardly pleasant, basically coarse and astonishingly favourable to Hitler. I sensed what was coming, wanted to get out of this plague-stricken country, but Franz Werfel clung doggedly to what he called "this last remnant of Europe" and didn't want to leave. We would have to pay dearly for that.'

All they were doing was putting off the evil day. They spent the winter in Paris, where Alma had the great good fortune to recover a treasure: the manuscript of Bruckner's Third Symphony. It was one of the things she had left in her trunk in Vienna for Carl Moll to look after. Hitler, an admirer of Bruckner, had let it be known that he wished to buy the manuscript, using Moll's son-in-law Eberstaller as intermediary. Faithful Ida got wind of the proposal, quietly removed the manuscript, packed it into a rough parcel and entrusted it to someone she knew was going to Paris. When the messenger discovered what the parcel contained, she delivered it to Alma. In Vienna, Eberstaller was hauled over the coals.

In her room in the Hotel Royal-Madeleine Alma tried to put her world together again. She invited some friends: Margherita Sarfatti, Mussolini's ex-mistress, now in a precarious situation, Bruno Walter, who had managed to get out of Germany in time, the poet Fritz von Unruh, the composer Darius Milhaud, the historian Emil Ludwig. She looked up her dear friend Gustave Charpentier, who smothered her in flowers, and Berta Zuckerkandl, who had been saved by her French friends. Paul Géraldy, for whom she had done translation, had alerted Paul Clemenceau who had alerted the French ambassador in Berlin, André François-Poncet, and he had obtained a French entry visa for her.

The Werfels returned to Sanary for the summer months. They were the last days of peace. 'Emigration is a dreadful illness', wrote Alma. 'Franz Werfel is completely shattered, an old man—and quite without hope.'

In September war was declared. They found themselves in an impossible situation. All foreigners became suspect overnight, and they were foreigners in a small town, with Czech passports, speaking French with an Austrian accent. Why did they hang on, instead of leaving France right away? Because it was hard to move on, always to keep on moving on. Because they could not know what was going to happen. Could anyone have known?

The day Belgium surrendered they were at their wits' end, hastily packed their bags, and hurried to Marseilles in the naïve hope of getting a boat for the United States. They didn't have a visa. German troops marched into Paris, spread out over the country, the French government fled to Bordeaux. They didn't know what to do . . . They tried to get to Bordeaux, by taxi. But they got no further than Carcassonne, where they were held up by a road-block.

At the railway station they had the absurd idea of handing in their luggage for registration to Bordeaux. A train came in. They managed to get on it. When they arrived, all was hurly-burly and confusion, their luggage was nowhere to be found. They didn't have a toothbrush between them. After a night in a brothel whose inmates had fled, they found a car which took them to Biarritz, whence they hoped to cross into Spain. The desperate hunt for Spanish visas began. Suddenly, while they were at lunch, someone said: 'The Germans are in Hendaye! You must leave at once!'

Off they went again, got to Pau, went on to Lourdes, which was swarming with refugees. They tried hotel after hotel and eventually found a hotel-keeper who took pity on these travellers without luggage. They wanted to return to Marseilles, but foreigners could no longer travel without permits.

During the days they spent at Lourdes, waiting for the military authorities to give them their travel permits, they discovered the miraculous grotto, and the story of Bernadette Soubirous. And Franz Werfel made a vow: 'If I get to America safe and sound, I'll write a book about Bernadette.' It seemed a faint hope. But at last they got their permits and slipped unobtrusively on to a train bound for Marseilles. Thanks to the perseverance and kindness of the hotel-keeper at Lourdes, they had finally recovered their luggage from some obscure depot, including even the precious valise containing the Bruckner and Mahler manuscripts.

In Marseilles, again crowded with refugees, they had a stroke of luck and found a room in a hotel. And once more there was a desperate hunt for a visa, hours spent in queues, the desperate running to and fro of trapped animals . . . After many tribulations, salvation appeared in the shape of the representative of the Emergency Rescue Committee, Varian Fry, who had been delegated by the United States government to provide help to distinguished refugees. Eleanor Roosevelt had intervened personally to obtain from her husband 'emergency' visas for a handful of artists, writers, and scientists.

Varian Fry now took charge of arrangements for the Werfels. They had an American visa entered on their passport. But it was impossible to get an exit visa from the French authorities. Indeed, under a clause of the armistice convention, France was under an obligation to hand over the refugees to the Germans. There was nothing the American could do about that.

So he decided to have the Werfels conducted clandestinely over the frontier into Spain, together with a trio of Germans who bore an illustrious name: Thomas Mann's son Golo, his brother Heinrich, and Nelly, the wife of the latter. They were not Jews—they were worse than that, so to speak. Hitler had put a curse on Thomas Mann. They set off from Cerbère, and followed a path used by many escapees until it was 'blown', since it crossed the Pyrenees over a relatively low ridge. A young American under Fry's orders guided the fugitives through boulders and bushes. Nelly Mann suddenly shouted that she didn't want to go on—it was Friday the 13th! They managed to calm her down.

The rest can be briefly told. Their long scramble over, they all arrived in Spain, where Fry was waiting for them with their luggage. They continued into Portugal, and one fine day found themselves on a Greek boat. They were saved! In New York, Klaus Mann, Thomas's eldest son, was waiting for them on the quayside. He watched a whole boatload of emigrant intellectuals from Germany and Austria come down the gangway, then found the group he was waiting for. They were all in good form, rested and sunburnt after their long sea voyage.

'Only Frau Alma seemed somewhat diminished,' he wrote later, 'every inch the fallen queen.' And that was to be her role from then on. Alma the queen had lost her kingdom for ever.

12. Mahler's Widow Once More

What followed? A life of emigrants among emigrants: the Manns, the Schönbergs, Bruno Walter, Erich Maria Remarque, and others less well-known. Seeing and being with each other, helping each other . . . The Werfels, like the others, chose to live in California. There at least the weather was fine.

They settled in a little house in Los Angeles, where Franz at once got down to work. Money was not an immediate problem since Alma still had some of the dollars Mahler had deposited in Lazards' bank in New York. And then came the miracle of Lourdes, if one dare call it that. In accordance with his vow Franz had written *The Song of Bernadette*. It was published and immediately became an enormous success. It was bought by the Book of the Month Club, Hollywood bought the film rights—overnight Franz Werfel became a well-known author in the United States.

He needed the success, poor fellow, for he found life as an emigrant very hard to bear. No one was more European, more utterly Viennese, than he. Then, against a background of the collapse of France, he wrote a brilliant comedy, *Jakobowsky and the Colonel*. They were not living badly under the Californian sun. They already had a new house, in Beverly Hills, which they had equipped with the essentials: books, a piano, and a black cook. But Alma wrote in her diary: 'Franz is tired and takes no pleasure in work. He is closed and dead. He needs a new love or a similar experience. That would be very painful for me, since I am completely wrapped up in him, and don't want—nor can I hope for—anything else.'

No, she couldn't hope for anything else. Even for Alma there were limits. It would have been a remarkable 'première' in her life if Franz had fallen in love with some young Hollywood lady, instead of her, Alma, being the betrayer, the unfaithful one, the executioner, as so often in the past. But she was not to be put to the test. Her tender little husband had no inclination in that direction, even if he did sometimes rebel when Alma pulled too hard on the reins and they indulged in one of those violent scenes from which she would emerge, refreshed, as after a good swim. He smoked too much. He drank too much. He did not possess, to make his exile bearable, that special strength which kept Alma going, that unshakeable conviction that the centre of the world was there where she happened to be.

Franz had a heart attack, then a second one, serious this time, which confined him to his bed and prevented him from attending the Hollywood première of the film of *The Song of Bernadette*. They listened instead to the radio broadcast of the occasion.

'I am terribly afraid of losing Franz Werfel', she wrote, but added, with typical frankness: 'In the evening he is tired and in the morning there is a bad smell about him that no wife ought to have to put up with.' No pity for the weak, ever. But she was no longer young and had no desire to change husbands. This time she knew that the one she had would be the last. So, without compassion, but efficiently, she looked after him.

The illness had made Franz temporarily incontinent, but he recovered and resumed writing a novel, *The Star of the Unborn*. On 25 August 1945 he sat down at his desk after lunch. Towards five o'clock Alma came to ask him if he would like a cup of tea. She knocked, he didn't reply, she went in and found him dead. He was 56. He had at least lived long enough to be able to rejoice at the news that Hitler's Germany was crushed.

He was buried, like the hero of his last novel, in a dinner jacket, a silk shirt with a second in reserve, his spectacles in his pocket. As he lay in his coffin in one of the lugubrious American funeral parlours, a distinguished company came to pay their respects: the Manns, Otto Klemperer, Igor Stravinsky, Otto Preminger, Bruno Walter, who played a piece by Schubert on the piano . . . Alma did not come.

Almost thirty years of life together, and now this brutal separation. But Alma would surmount that too. Manon's judgement of her mother was not mistaken. Alma was 66, was increasingly deaf, drank a whole bottle of Benedictine every day, had had three husbands, four children, and was now alone, alone. It was hard.

Franz Werfel's elder sister disputed the will which made Alma the sole beneficiary of all Franz's author's rights: she lost her case. Alma was not exactly wealthy, but she would never be in need. The radio broadcast a report that Franz Werfel's widow was going to marry Bruno Walter. She haughtily denied 'this joke in bad taste'. Bruno Walter walked across the lawn that separated their two houses in Beverly Hills, and said, with a chuckle: 'Well, would it be so terrible?' Alma threw him out.

She injured her right hand. A friend sent her Scriabin's piano pieces for the left hand, and she applied herself with enthusiasm to them. She received from London a request for help from the Dutch conductor Willem Mengelberg. He had in his possession the manuscripts of Mahler's Fourth Symphony and the final movement of the *Song of the Earth*, and needed to sell them. Alma wouldn't hear of it. Mengelberg's financial predicament was no concern of hers.

One day, having acquired American nationality, she took a plane for Europe, Plato in one pocket, a flask of Benedictine in the other. She stopped off in London to see Anna—who was soon to leave her fourth husband—found her prematurely aged, found her granddaughter ugly, and went off again. She had never loved, really loved, her children, except Manon, who flattered her vanity. She loved her grandchildren even less. Being a grandmother was not for her.

From London she went to Vienna. She wanted to see it again. She was horrified to find the Opera, the Burgtheater, the cathedral, all in ruins. She found no one she knew in the town, except for her old maidservant, and Alban Berg's widow, Helene, who was now only interested in spiritualism. The top floor of the house on the Hohe Warte, where Mahler's and Werfel's worktables had stood, had been destroyed by American bombs. The house on the Semmering, sold to the Soviet authorities, had been 'redecorated', Kokoschka's fresco had been whitewashed over.

Carl Moll had sold everything she had asked him to keep for her, including the famous picture by Munch, *The Midnight Sun*. He had committed suicide, with his daughter and son-in-law, the day the Red Army entered Vienna. What infuriated Alma was the attitude of the civil servants and lawyers to whom she went to try and recover her possessions. They were all, in 1947, Nazis. The guilty one, in their eyes, was not Carl Moll but Alma, since she had married two Jews.

So she left, outraged. An American lawyer would try to recuperate what he could. Vienna, for Alma, was struck off the map. She returned later to Europe, to Paris, to Rome, but never to Vienna.

In spite of the loneliness of her life after Franz's death, she seems in some sense to have been delivered. No more husbands, no more lovers, no more creative works to nurture—those ferocious little beasts which sucked your blood—no more constraints, free, at last. So, music: could she compose at last? It was too late. Often in the past few years she had improvised at the piano, she was very good at that. But composing was something else, it meant work, a technique, a discipline. Alma never resumed her interrupted dream. She had asserted herself (and how forcefully!) but through her dominance over men, not by her own creativity. She had only been allowed to cultivate one art, that of being loved. Someone, somewhere, had been murdered, and the corpse's blood had irrigated the fields that others ploughed. She was now going to spend the remaining years of her life in a noble role: that of the Widow.

Settled in New York in one of the three apartments which she now owned (she was a tightfisted landlady), waited on by the faithful Ida whom she had brought over from Austria, she had reconstituted her stage setting: a library and a music room, her portrait by Kokoschka, the portrait of Mahler on the piano, works of art in profusion. She had so many that she didn't know where to put them. She gave some away. A Klee to Stravinsky for example. At the time it wasn't worth anything.

Always in black, but covered in jewellery, the tenacious old lady played up the part of 'Mahler's widow' for all she was worth, because her first husband's music was beginning to come into vogue, and gradually phased out her role as 'Werfel's widow', because her third husband's public was diminishing. Mischievous onlookers dubbed her 'the widow of the Four Arts'.

She sorted through her papers, made copies of Franz's letters, corrected and expurgated her diary, burnt, destroyed, wrote memoirs. Her daughter Anna now lived in the United States, but in California, so that she was still as far away as when she had lived in Europe. Alma continued to occupy a certain position in the musical community. In

1959 Benjamin Britten asked her permission to dedicate his 'Nocturne for Tenor and Small Orchestra' to her. She was guest of honour at all concerts in which Mahler was part of the programme, attended rehearsals, went to dinner at Leonard Bernstein's, invited Georg Solti and his wife to her place . . . She had become an institution.

And there were a chosen few whom she let know that she expected them to come and see her. And they came. Gropius came to see her whenever he was in New York. And one day a note arrived from Kokoschka: he was there, he wanted to see her. She hesitated. And then she said no. And she was right. You don't show your ravaged countenance to a man who has loved you in all your glory. Whereupon Kokoschka sent her this telegram, the last: 'Dear Alma, in my *Windsbraut* we are for ever united.' She had been more than the love of his life, she had been his light, his passion, his sun.

One evening, alone, she pondered on the little group of men she had had at her feet. And she reached this conclusion: 'I never really liked Mahler's music, I was never really interested in what Werfel wrote' (and never, she might have added, really understood what Gropius was doing), 'but Kokoschka, yes, Kokoschka always impressed me.' No doubt about it, in that handful of aces Kokoschka was the ace of hearts—always supposing hearts meant anything to Alma. But when the final trick had been played she was, and would for ever remain, Alma Mahler.

The siren with the blue eyes died of pneumonia on 11 December 1964, at the age of 85, clasping her daughter's hand. For the last year her mind had been confused. She was suffering from diabetes but refused to have treatment on the grounds that it was a 'Jewish illness' which she couldn't possibly have.

Should she be buried in California with Franz Werfel? Or in Austria with Gustav Mahler? In accordance with her own wish, as reported by her maid, it was with Manon, in the cemetery at Grinzing, that Alma was to share the peace of eternity.

Now, in her prison of stone, there was no longer any room for arrogance.

BIBLIOGRAPHY

The chapters in this book dealing with Alma's first marriage are based largely on the monumental study of Mahler by his principal biographer Henry-Louis de La Grange: *Gustav Mahler*, 3 vols. (Paris: Fayard, 1983). Other sources which have been consulted are listed below.

The Alma Mahler–Werfel Collection in the Charles Patterson van Pelt library of the University of Pennsylvania, Pa.

CANETTI, ELIAS, *Das Augenspiel: Lebensgeschichte 1931–37* (Munich and Vienna: Karl Hanser Verlag, 1985).

GRANGE, HENRY LOUIS DE LA, *Gustav Mahler*, Eng. trans. of vol. i only (London: Gollancz, 1974).

ISAACS, REGINALD, *Walter Gropius, ein Mensch und seine Werk* (Berlin: Mann, 1983).

JOHNSTON, WILLIAM M., *The Austrian Mind: An Intellectual and Social History* (Berkeley, Calif.: University of California Press, 1976).

JONES, ERNEST, *The Life and Work of Sigmund Freud* (New York: Doubleday, 1955).

JUNGK, P. S., *Franz Werfel: Eine Lebensgeschichte* (Frankfurt-am-Main: S. Fischer, 1987).

KOKOSCHKA, OSKAR, *My Life*, tr. David Britt (London: Thames and Hudson, 1974).

—— *Briefe IV 1953–1976* (Düsseldorf: Classen, 1988).

KRAUS, KARL, *Sprüche und Widersprüche* (Vienna and Leipzig, 'Die Fackel', 1924).

MAHLER, ALMA, *Mein Leben* (Frankfurt-am-Main: S. Fischer, 1960).

—— *Gustav Mahler, M—ories and Letters*, ed. Donald Mitchell and Knud Martner, tr. Basil Creighton, 4th edn. (London: Sphere Books, 1990).

—— and ASHTON, E. B., *And the Bridge is Love* (London: Hutchinson, 1959).

MANN, KLAUS, *The Turning Point: The Autobiography of Klaus Mann* (London: Serpent's Tail, 1987).

MAYSEL, LUCIAN, *La Femme de Vienne* (Paris: Le Chemin Vert, 1987).

MONSON, KAREN, *Alma Mahler: Muse to Genius* (London: Collins, 1984).

POLLAK, MICHAEL, *Vienne, 1900* (Paris: Archives, Gallimard, 1986).

REIK, THEODOR, *Variations psychanalytiques sur un thème de Mahler* (Paris: Denoël, 1972).

SCHORSKE, CARL E., *Fin-de-Siècle Vienna: Politics and Culture* (London: Weidenfeld & Nicolson, 1980).

WERFEL, FRANZ, *Cella oder die Uberwinder*, in Franz Werfel, *Erzählungen aus Zwei Welten*, iii (Frankfurt-am-Main: S. Fischer, 1954).

WHITFORD, FRANK, *Bauhaus* (London: Thames and Hudson, 1984).

ZUCKERKANDL, BERTHA, *Osterreich intim: Erinnerungen 1890–1942* (Frankfurt-am-Main: Propyläen, 1970).

ZWEIG, STEFAN, *The World of Yesterday: An Autobiography* (London: Cassell, 1943).

INDEX